To Gerry

Best Wishes

[illegible]

Lavenham

2022

# THE EAST SEAXE

TWO PERSONAL VIEWS OF ESSEX
IN POETRY AND PHOTOGRAPHS

**ROBERT HALLMANN & MERVYN LINFORD**

**LITTORAL PRESS**

First published in 2017 by:
The Littoral Press, 15 Harwood Place,
Lavenham, Suffolk CO10 9SG

ISBN 978-1-912412-01-3



British Library Cataloguing-in-Publication Data:
A catalogue record of this book is available from the British Library



Printed by: 4 Edge Ltd. Hockley, Essex

**Foreword: ML**

Although I now live just across the border in Lavenham, Suffolk, in truth, I'm an Essex man. Perhaps not born and bred but I lived in Pitsea for eighteen years, Southend on Sea for thirty eight years, and Coggeshall, Maylandsea and Great Bardfield for two years each. That's a sum total of sixty two years altogether. I also lived in Sudbury, Suffolk, for three years and as I looked out of my study window across the River Stour and its attendant water meadows, the rising ground that I beheld, was Essex at its wooded and rolling finest. Even now I spend approximately half of my time at my partner's house in Leigh on Sea, so I'm still heavily involved with my formative land and seascapes.

The county is much maligned and demeaned by those who are obviously not as well acquainted with its topography as I am. Flat is the usual derogatory epithet. Not true - not true. Perhaps in part, somewhat like 'the curate's egg' but only in part. Close to Langley in the north west of the county the hills rise to well over four hundred feet, and even further south at Danbury and Langdon Hills altitudes of over three hundred and fifty feet are not uncommon. The southerly extent of the last Ice Age follows a line north east, south west which is roughly comparable to the route of the A12 from Colchester to Chelmsford. I'm no geologist but I've always felt that there is a subtle difference both north and south of the A12 - chalky boulder clay to the north perhaps, and glacial sands and gravels more prevalent to the south. To me personally, in many ways it feels like two different counties. I say feel, because it's as much a feeling as a fact I should imagine. It's a subtle difference to be found in the flora and fauna and sometimes in the slightly divergent farming practices.

What is noticeable as one travels around Essex is that although the east of the county borders the sea, the estuaries, rivers and creeks associated with the 'German Ocean' - as the North Sea was once known - spread their maritime influence right into the heart of the Essex countryside. Essex has some 450 kilometres of seawall which is more than any other county in England. As much as I love the countryside of North Essex and South Suffolk where I now live, I am a marsh man at heart. The half-timbered villages and thatched cottages are one thing - and I've lived in and thoroughly enjoyed such chocolate box environments, but it's the estuaries, the creeks and the saltings that inspire my creative and imaginative pursuits - my poetry and my prose writing.

Whereas most areas of the British Isles have been substantially altered by the needs of mankind, those areas of salt marsh, saltings, creeks, gullies and mudflats below the seawalls are still as close to really wild as we can get. As a boy by the marshes at Pitsea, Vange, Fobbing, Bowers Gifford, Benfleet, Leigh and Canvey, and as an adult further afield in estuaries of Essex and Suffolk: Crouch, Blackwater, Colne, Stour, Orwell, Alde, Ore, Blyth and Deben, I have found that by some means of environmental osmosis these places have become an integral part of my being. I don't in effect write about them - they in fact, write me.

Most of my poetry and prose is nature orientated. I'm as obsessed by the weather as I am by the flora and the fauna of Essex and Suffolk, but I'm also interested in its agriculture, its local history, the arts, poetry and literature. I have known my co-author, Robert Hallmann, for many years. We are both members of the same writer's group and give talks and readings of and about our respective books.

Robert's poetry is mostly rhymed and traditional and mine is for the most part written as 'free verse'. The reasoning behind this collaboration was that the traditional verse would draw people in - especially children and that that might then encourage them to read the more modern poems of mine. My belief as a poet and writer is that both modern and traditional works of literature are of equal importance.

**Mervyn Linford, Lavenham, Suffolk**

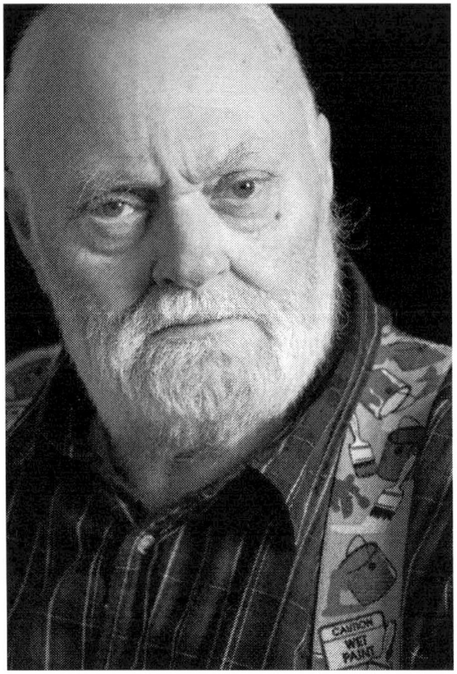

**Mervyn Linford**

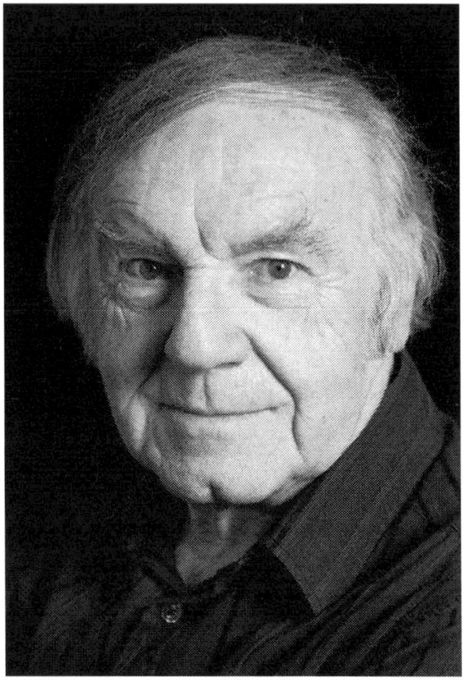

**Robert Hallmann**

**Foreword RH**

Born far inland in Continental Europe, it was not until I left home at the age of 20 that I faced the expanse of the open sea for the first time. That was in Holland. Employment in Wales, England and Ireland followed until I settled in London instead of returning to Germany as planned. I was a typesetter in the traditional Gutenberg sense. Switching to typographer and designer in the West End, I settled and became a commuter.

The landlocked southern tip of Westphalia, the rural Sauerland also known as 'the land of a thousand hills', is so different from Essex it is surprising – even to me – that I settled in a land where the gentle sides of rivers or former rivers are seen as steep and ridges in the landscape are termed hills. There is, however, the familiarity of a Saxon presence in many of the local place names that tie our history together.

Nowhere are we far from the sea in the land of the East Seaxe and that sea has undecided convoluting borders. Estuary fluctuates with the tides at the pull of the moon. That governs the outline of the land, the width of rivers as they empty into the sea and produce shelves of alluvial mud that would seem impenetrable at low tide. At high tide much of the land vanishes and re-joins the sea, but that sea can also assert its awesome power over land that can be conquered and inundated at great distress.

Over the years this natural landscape must have crept into my soul, as I began to photograph it, research its past and write about it first in magazine articles and then in books. I shared it in exhibitions and in verse. Sometimes history fuses with the landscape, one stumbles into it and its people become familiar again, re-emerging from written accounts and documents. The veneer of modernity is only skin deep.

And in that landscape, through the seasons, the weather and the views you may be filled with emotions that simply have to be noted down and what better way to crystallise them than in verse. My idea of poetry may be seen as old fashioned by many. Let the words speak for themselves.

When Mervyn Linford suggested a collaboration it did not take long for me to agree, a poet I admire, who also thinks about land and environment in his own illustrious way. I trust my photographs underline that Essex sense of place. Can a man have two homes? Love two places with equal passion? Why not, if the heart be big enough?

**Robert Hallmann, Hadleigh, Essex**

**CONTENTS**

**LIST OF ILLUSTRATIONS**

## FERRYMAN
(At North Fambridge)

Along the shore, by tides decayed
Slim sentinels parade, un-swayed,
Black dragons' teeth in gums of mud
Once stood at bay the hostile flood.
The core of ancient earthworks' might
With hazel wove held back the tide.

The tides have won and worn them down,
Those guardians black, that limpets crown.
And seaweed strands like widows' weeds
Sway darkly in the summer breeze
From ribs of boats that time forgot,
Degrading in their muddy cot.

Be still and listen for the shout –
Across the Crouch a bell rings out.
In rain or shine, in wind and squall
Strong arms pull oars to heed the call.
The ferryman's stout, unfailing toil
Brought travellers safe to Dengie soil.

You hear that bell some winter's night,
See lantern-swayed unsteady light,
Hear eerie splash of ghostly oars
Across the deep, when north wind roars…
And sense the ferryman bid 'God speed'
Close by the Ferry Boat Inn retreat.

RH

## SUNSET
(Creeksea)

Where the tide
has spilled across the road
puddles reflect the sky:

sky and the rusted purslane
    and the moon -
that cold and skull-like, gibbous
smudge of white that speaks of stars.

    Here on green-encrusted ropes
Bladder-wrack is black and hung awry
where water once upheld it to the light
        in silver strands.

The double deeps hold wings
    as cormorant fly

and on the river's misted other side
where seals and mullet meet and multiply
    the sun explodes.

ML

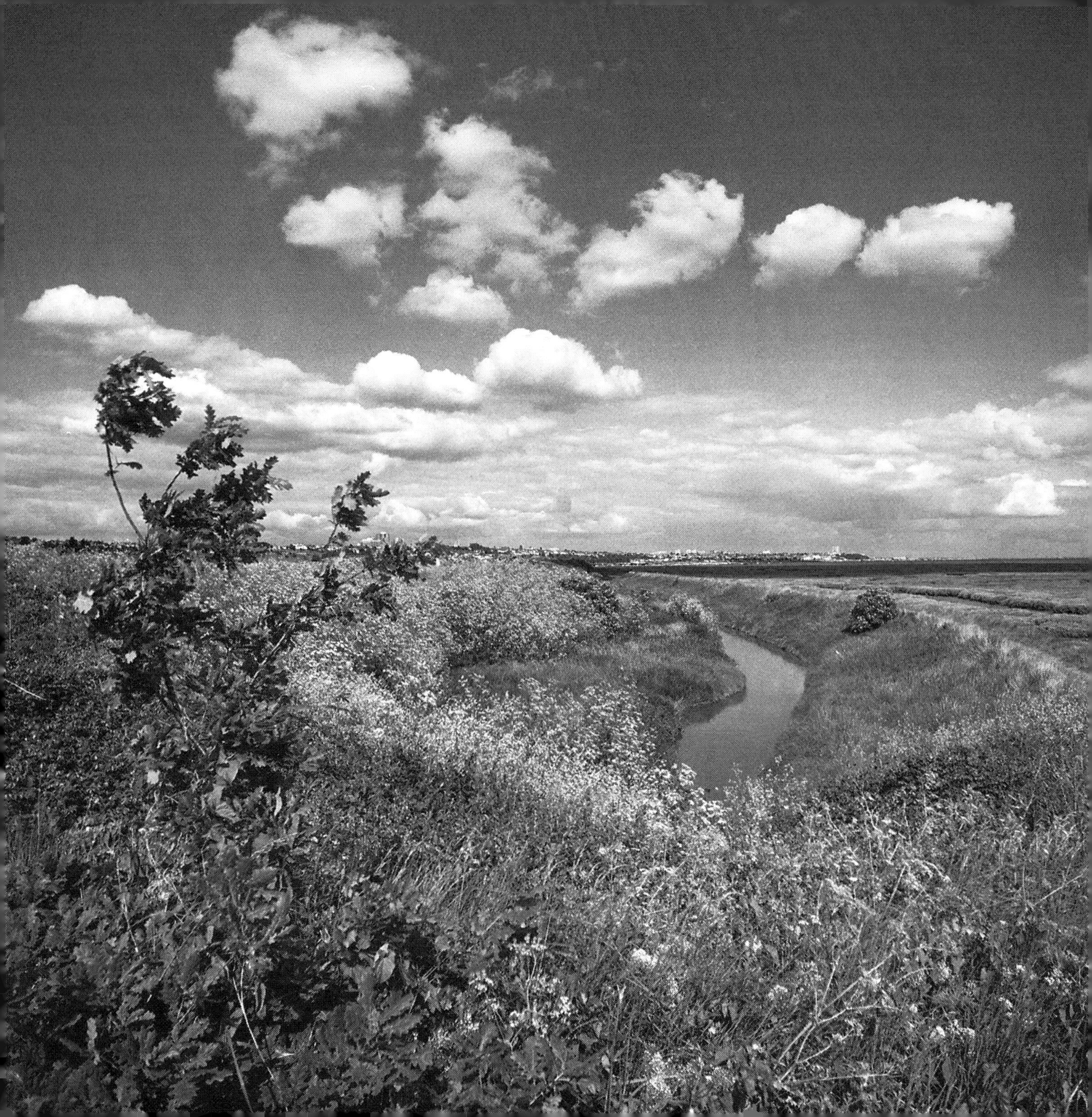

## BUTTERFLIES

When I was Spring, I used to like to dance.
A care-free ring-o'roses round the tree of May.
We'd hold our hands and skip and leap and prance
And mimic butterflies that live for one short day.

When I was summer, there was little time
And dance was a relief from hectic life.
The daily toil, success and cheer to mime,
We were the butterflies that danced, just to survive.

Now I am Autumn, in a measured stance
With simple joys, I hear the robin sing.
No more for me exhaustion of the dance.
I watch the butterflies in their ephemeral fling.

RH

## ESSEX SKIPPERS

Trying now to remember those fields where I as
a child stared into the sky amongst the flowers
    is never easy.

I can see in my mind's eye the vetches
and the willow herb and poppies
but time has taken something from the light
    that was my vision.

I cannot see or feel such fleeting things
as burnet moths or lizards or the wings
    of Essex skippers.

Images it seems are not enough
I need the actual touch that words can't bring
of butterflies between the cupping hands

whose gentle tickling beat is like a heart
that leaves behind a powder and the mark
    of all ephemera.

ML

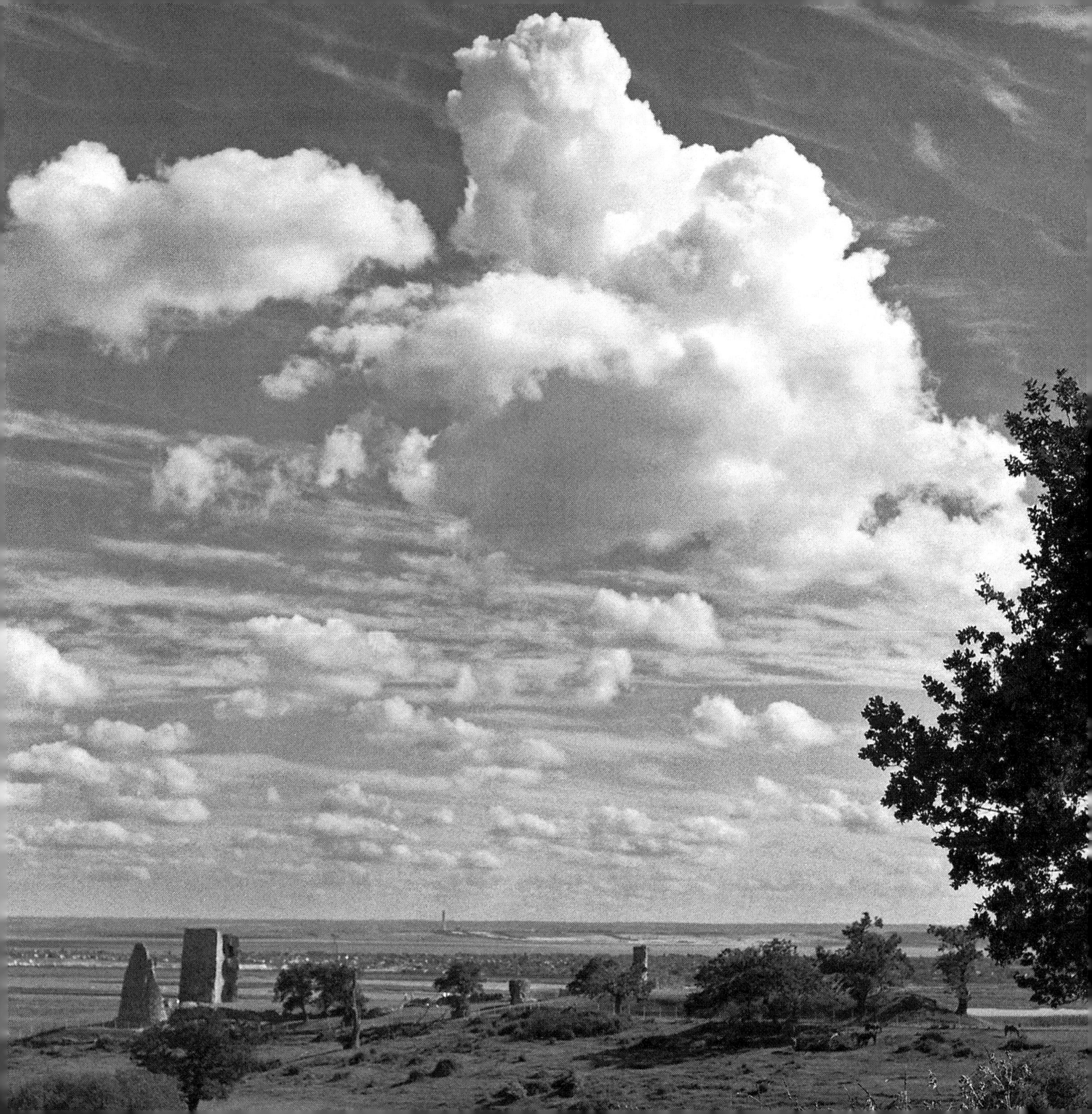

## CANVEY LIGHTS

When mists shroud blue the Essex shore,
When sapphire cloaks the leas,
Hushed Canvey, as a pool of lights
Floats on ethereal seas

While past it travel ship-shape stars
Both west and east, but slow –
A seamless canvas, pricked and pierced
Where tiny lanterns glow.

And all the marsh and merchant lands
Deem vanished from our sight.
The twilight of a perfect day
Glides to a star-crossed night…

RH

## HADLEIGH CASTLE

Out of sequence
with a world's events
these fragments
of eroded ragstone.

Histories of a far-off Kent
playing out their pageants on
an Essex shore.

Pockets of alien rock
lodged in the drift
of vestigial sands -

like knots in the land's long
memory
reminding the tide
of an alluvial obstinacy.

ML

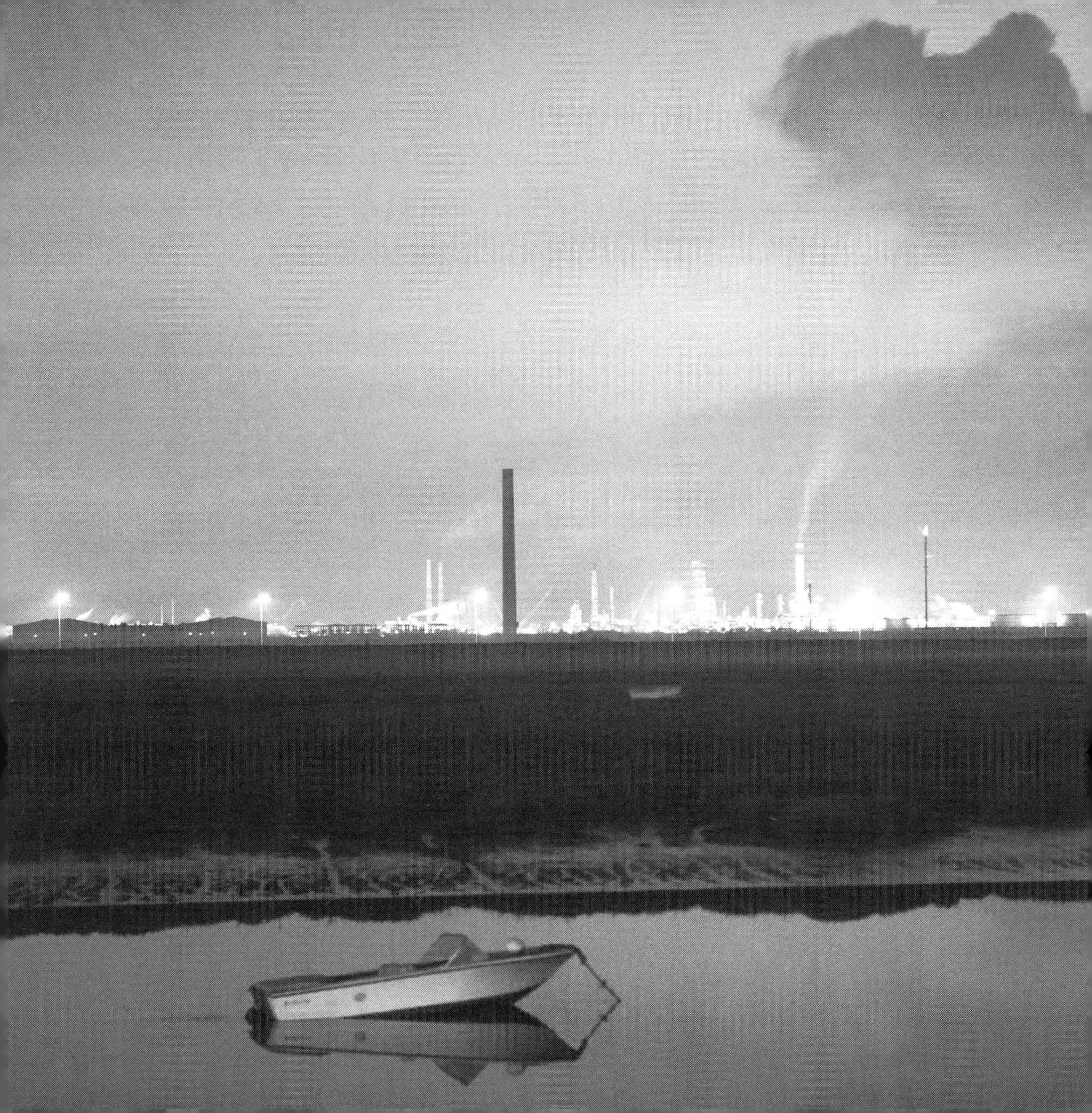

## PEREGRINE OVER CANVEY POINT

Canvey Point:
the point at the sea-surrounding island's end
glows in the early sunlight, like a finger -
a finger pointing southwards, who knows why,
to the shores of Kent.

My eyes in the dawn-light linger for a while
as the sea-mews cry and the skeins of geese returning
write their unwritten language and lament
for the end of summer.

The year is spent like the golden coins that glitter
out on the Yantlet Dredge and the gilded Ray
and the Crowstone points its own unbidden finger
up into skies where the snow and frost ferments
and a falcon flickers.

Try as they might the waders cannot dodge
the weather's loop, the seasons as they spin,
and although they lodge a protest as they fly
in alternating slants of dark and light
the feather's stooping moment will reply
without a word.

ML

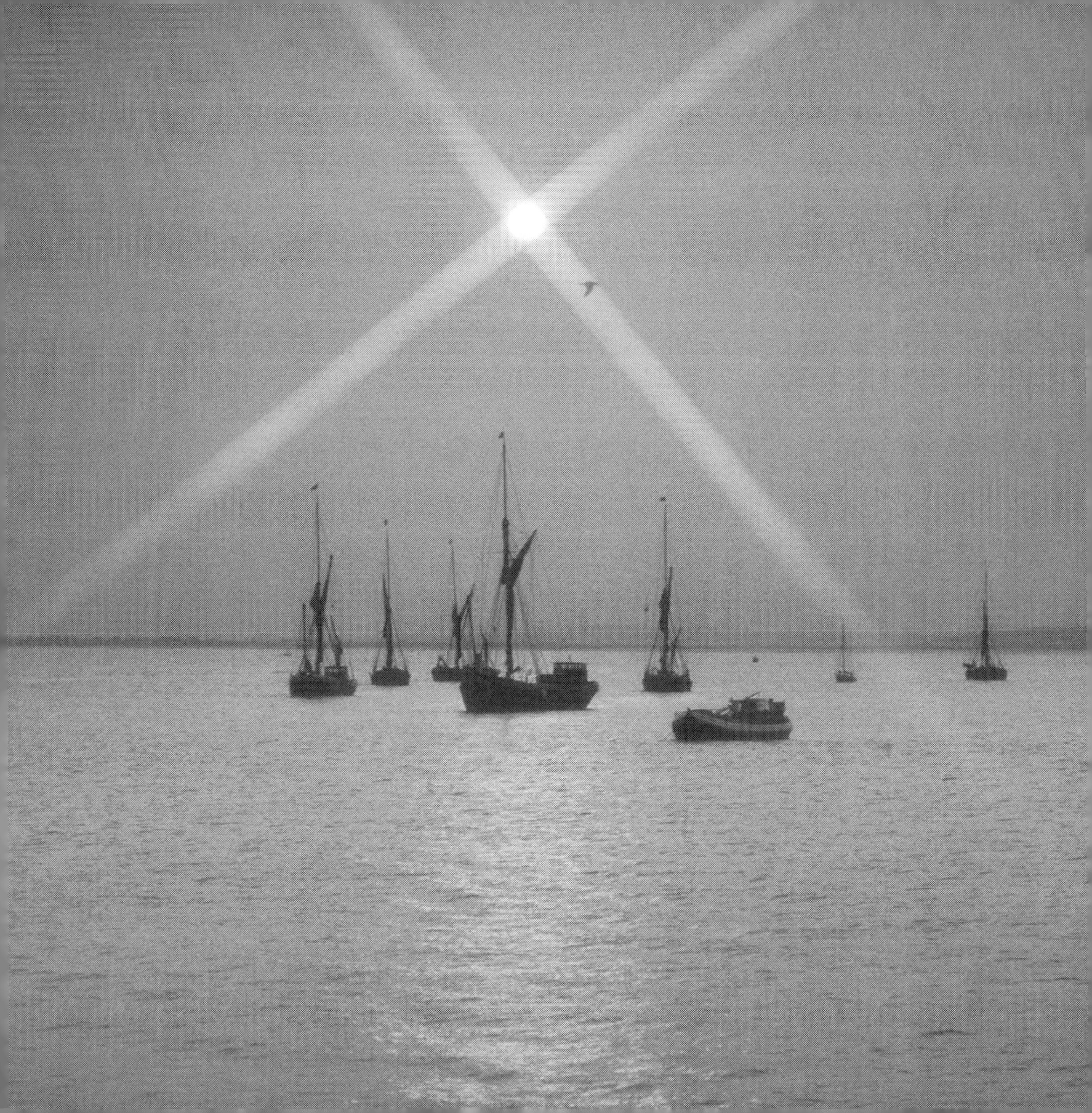

## CANVEY'S LOVELORN VIKING

Dare I, from a past dimension,
Reach across the gulf of time,
With a trembling hand's extension
Touch your heart and make you mine?
Once, I thirsted for adventure.
Once, I lived by axe and sword –
Made with plunder my indenture,
Greedy for my looted hoard:-

> Yet another maid to ravish.
> Yet another skull to crack.
> Yet another land to conquer.
> Yet another town to sack.

Now I haunt these lonely marshes,
Restless phantom of the Ray,
Searching for a Saxon maiden.
Lost my head. My ship. My way…
How I loathe the wild blue yonder.
Empty wastelands are my lot.
Without you, my fair companion,
Just a soul that time forgot.

> There are no more lands to conquer,
> There are no more towns to sack –
> Searching for that one fair maiden,
> Ever doomed to looking back.

RH

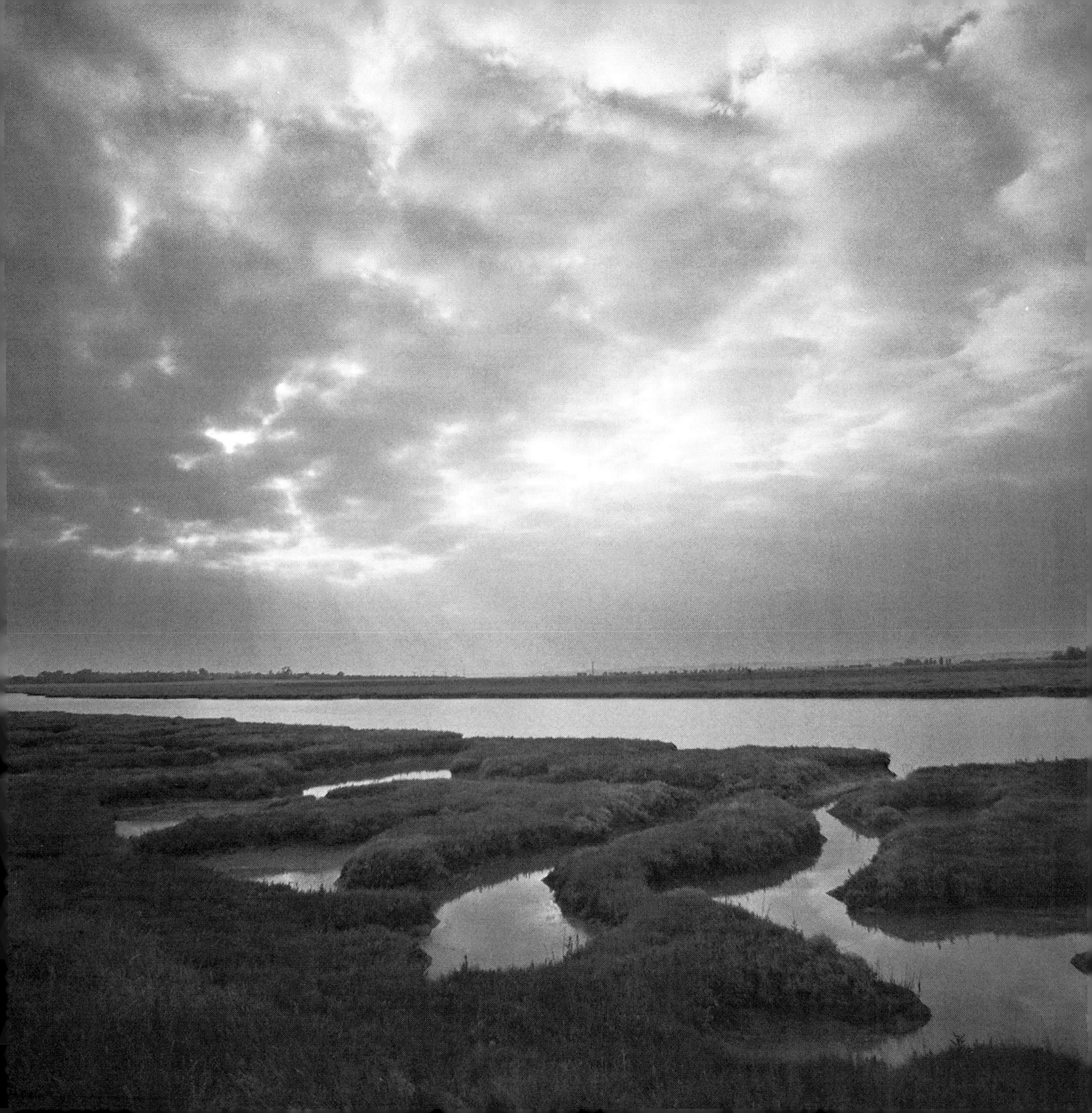

## THE SWALE

Out there beyond the Yantlet,
the Middle Grounds, the Medway and Sheppy,
we find the Swale.

Wider than your average creek and less sinuous
it cleaves the earth between the sea and downs
and leads the way to Thanet and the dead.

Before the ingenuity of man
with buoys and charts
to lead us up the Thames

this corridor of ooze and pewter tides
saw Roman galleys hauling flocks of gulls
without the curse of keels to run aground
before Londinium.

Celts and Romans, Saxon and Dane,
Jutes and Normans:

This route has seen them all
and here this Sunday morning in the sun
with mist across the mudflats and the geese
whose own migrations teach us how
to wonder and surmise
I preach again the primacy of words.

This ink that flows across the written page
as I, although inspired, start to ebb
will capture time like flounders in a net

and history – yes yours – and even mine
will be the sounds of seabirds in the west
as Venus climbs above Canary Wharf
and fades and founders. ML

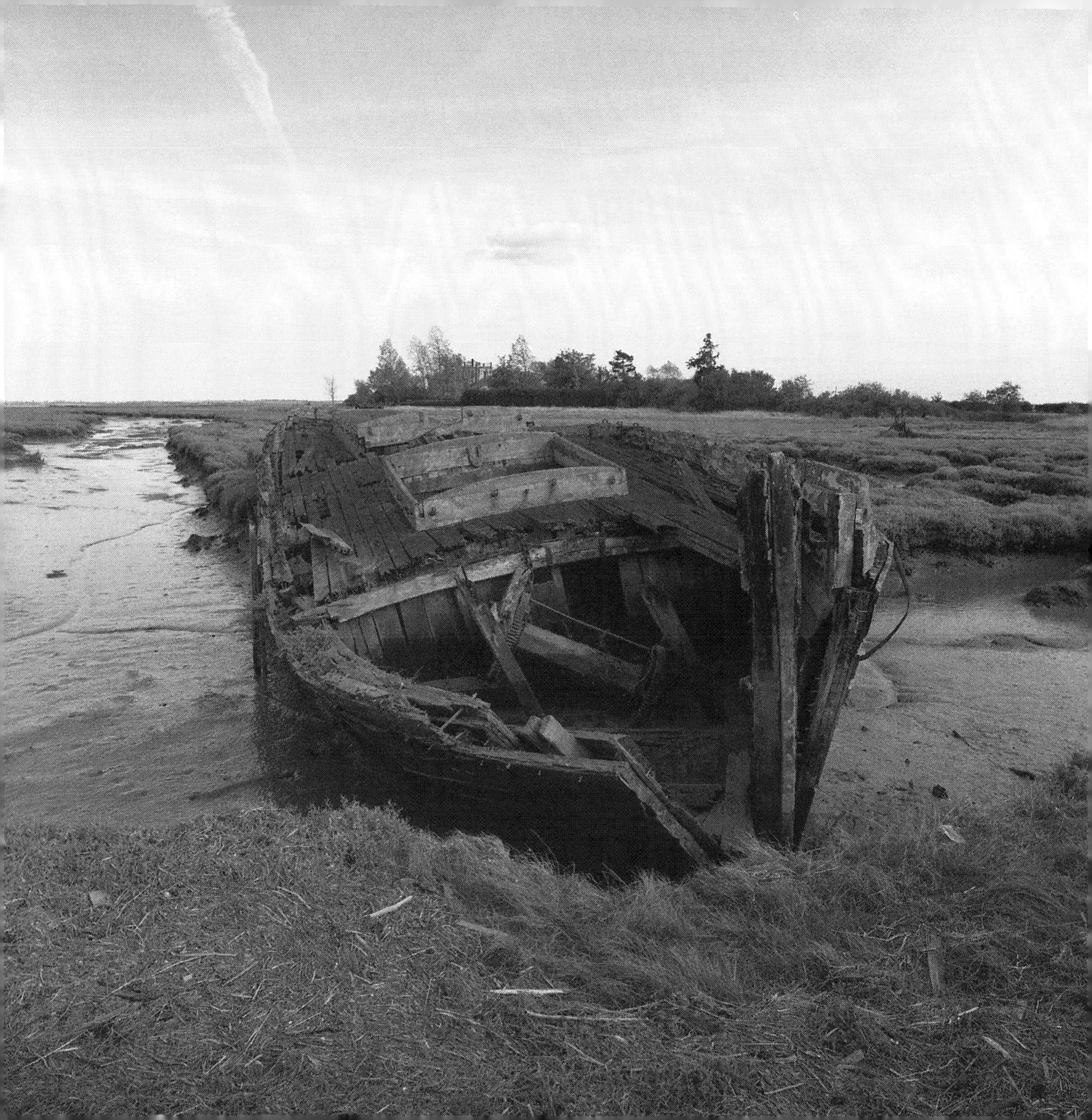

## CONTINUITY

Explore with me the quiet land.
Let Celt and Saxon take your hand.
Let Vikings make their bloody stand
And Kings ride by your side.

Retreat to Cedd's enduring hall
Across the Romans' warlike wall
And hear the Gospel's early call –
The chant of thousand years.

Then touch the ancient mason's mark,
The cut of adze, the beam stained dark
By pious torch of pitch and bark –
And feel the pulsing tide…

Of Norman zeal. Of castles strong.
Of churches high. Of evensong.
Of monks' communal, cloistered throng.
Of peasants' joys and tears.

Where'er you walk, on land or shore,
Another walked that way before,
Another built the passage door
Through which your steps resound…

The common bonds that weld a land
And weave its future strand by strand
Relentless, like the running sand
Of time, will hold you bound.

RH

## ESSEX SALTINGS

First time for decades they say –
ice in great white plates
turning the saltings into thoughts of tundra.

Memories of past millennia –
of lands created at the frozen edge.

The teal cut coldly on a wedge of wings –
burning the substance of their own survival.

A thought swings northwards through
          a nerve of air –
touching the sinews of another age.

Notions of despairing tribes
skirting the limits of a vast moraine,
with the far blue distance carved by serrations
   into slope and summit.

A curlew flutes its glacial refrain
and time's slow music melts to the moment
   and the mind's erosion.

ML

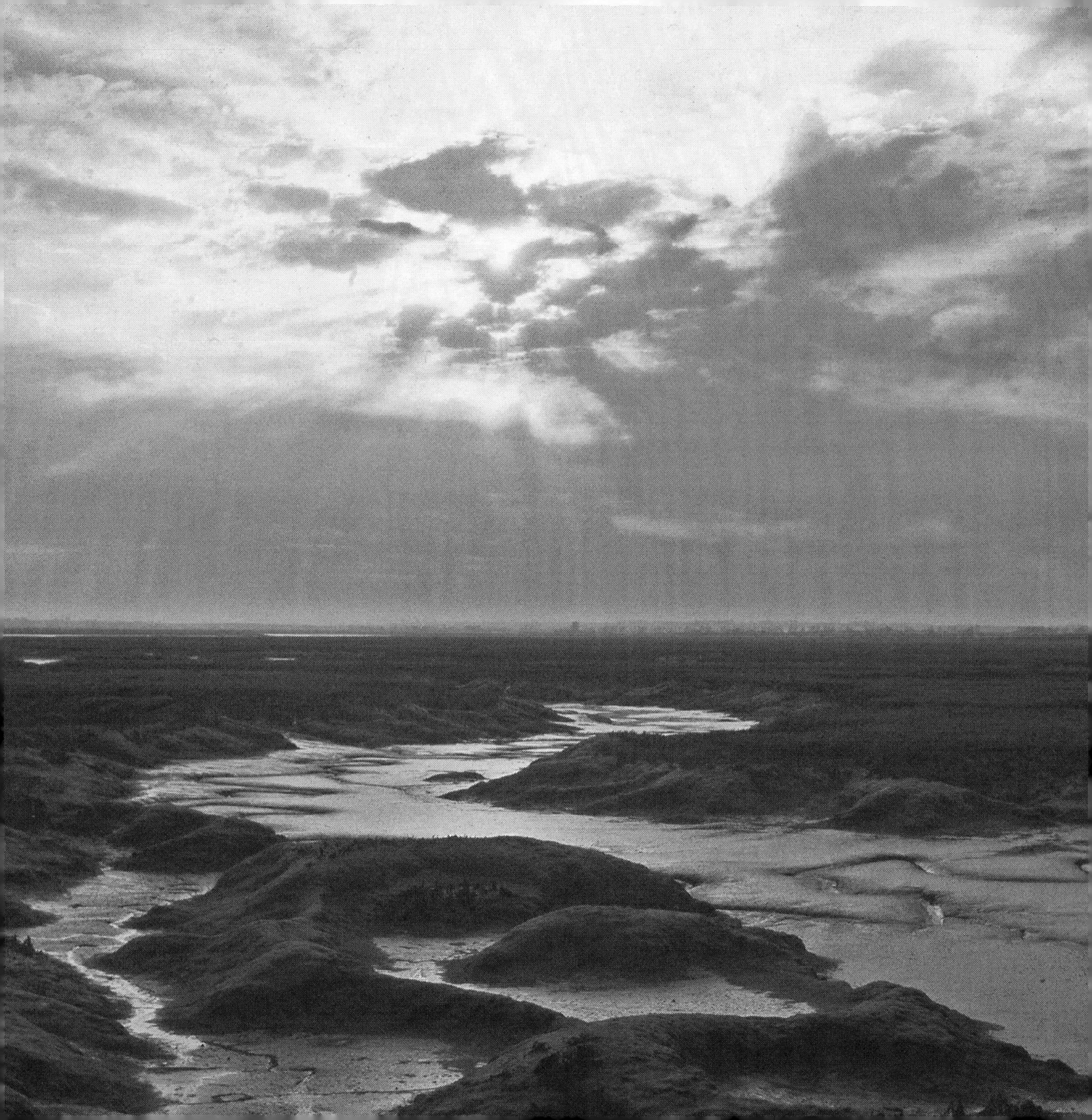

## COPT HALL MARSH

(Nat. Trust)

Relishing its evening glory,
Dipping gold the treacherous moat,
Sets the sun across the half-land,
Sinking in her sky-borne boat.

One last fling. With rays of wonder
Mirrored in the wet domain,
Goose and avocet and plover
View such portent with disdain.

Skylark flaunts its Jubilate,
Trills its worship to the sky
Landside, where the shadows lengthen –
One last Amen from on high.

Heedless of my transient footsteps,
Ducks in threes at evening flight
Circumnavigate the marshes,
Heading for the still of night…

RH

## TURNSTONES AFTER DAWN

The tide is high, the sun is up,
the turnstones as they twist and turn
    awry on gilded wings
        resemble fire.

They flicker, flare, erupt, like flying sparks,
    or settle on the shingle
        out of air
    like ash and embers.

The wavelets glint and sparkle on the shore:
riddle the glowing amber in the grate -
the coals of shifting shingle
and the flames

as every rushing phoenix, here and there,
across the hot inferno of the beach
lifts up as one in sunlight and the glare
    of an open door

October's unexpected summer furnace
courtesy of Luke and the Azores
as the turnstones twist and turn,
like an autumn prayer that spits
        and sputters.

ML

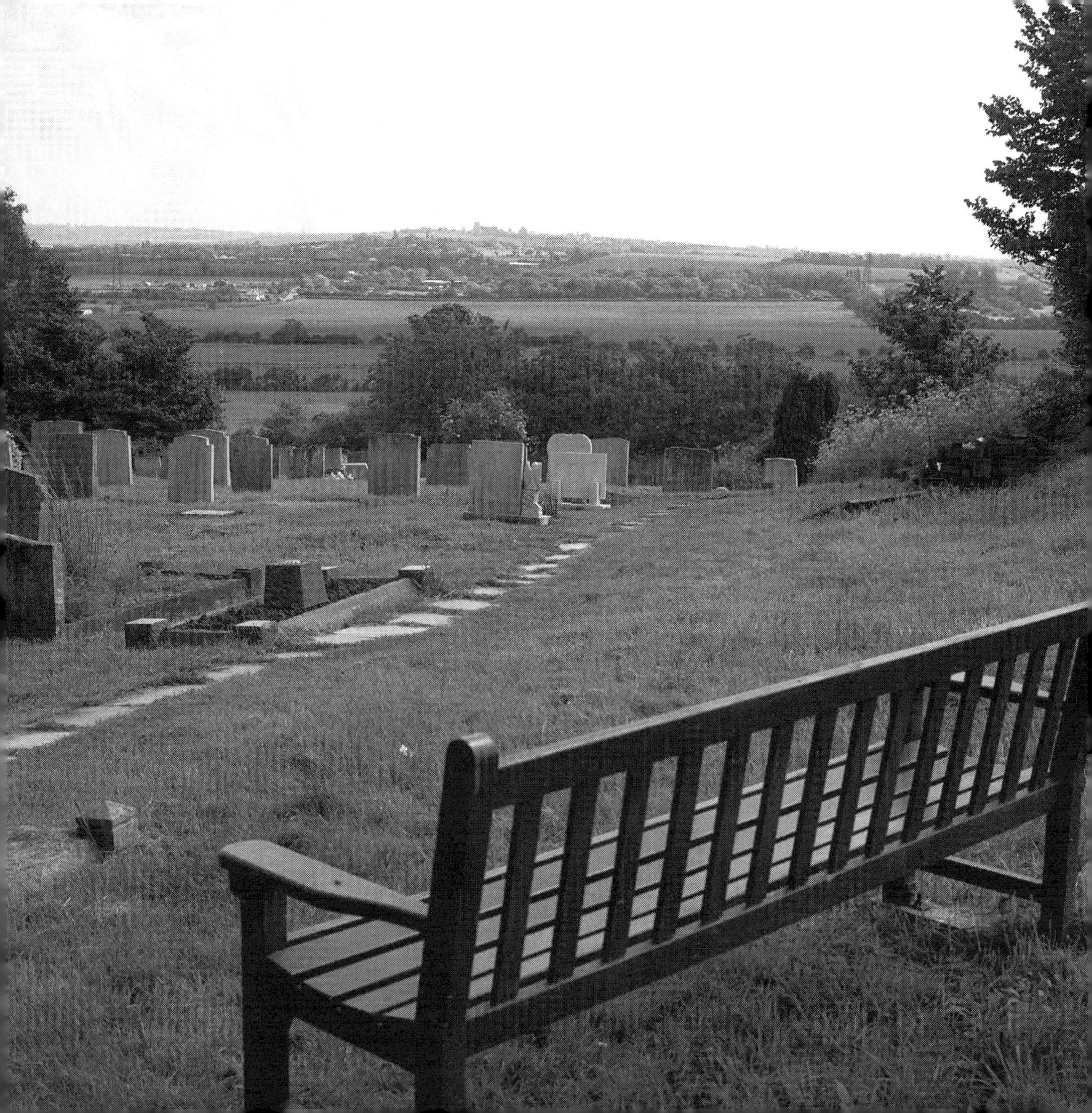

## EVENING FLIGHT ON THE CROUCH

Where the earth and the sea fight a battle harsh
On the high-tide mark, at the Fambridge Marsh
I stood quite alone on the edge of the land,
Feeling small, like eternity's ampersand
While the river rolled lazily by.

And I stood and watched with amazement and awe
As wave after wave in a steady flow
The geese rose into the changing light
In a surging crescendo of evening flight –
A gift and delight to the eye.

In ribbons strung out with wings touching wings,
Formations, like bunting on aerial strings,
They chattered and nattered and fluttered on high
All over that beautiful sun-setting sky
In a spell to the moment bound.

And I stood quite alone on the river's bank
Reflecting on riches, on wealth and rank.
Just me and the geese in an Essex night,
Fused into the wonders of time and tide –
Delighted by sight and sound.

RH

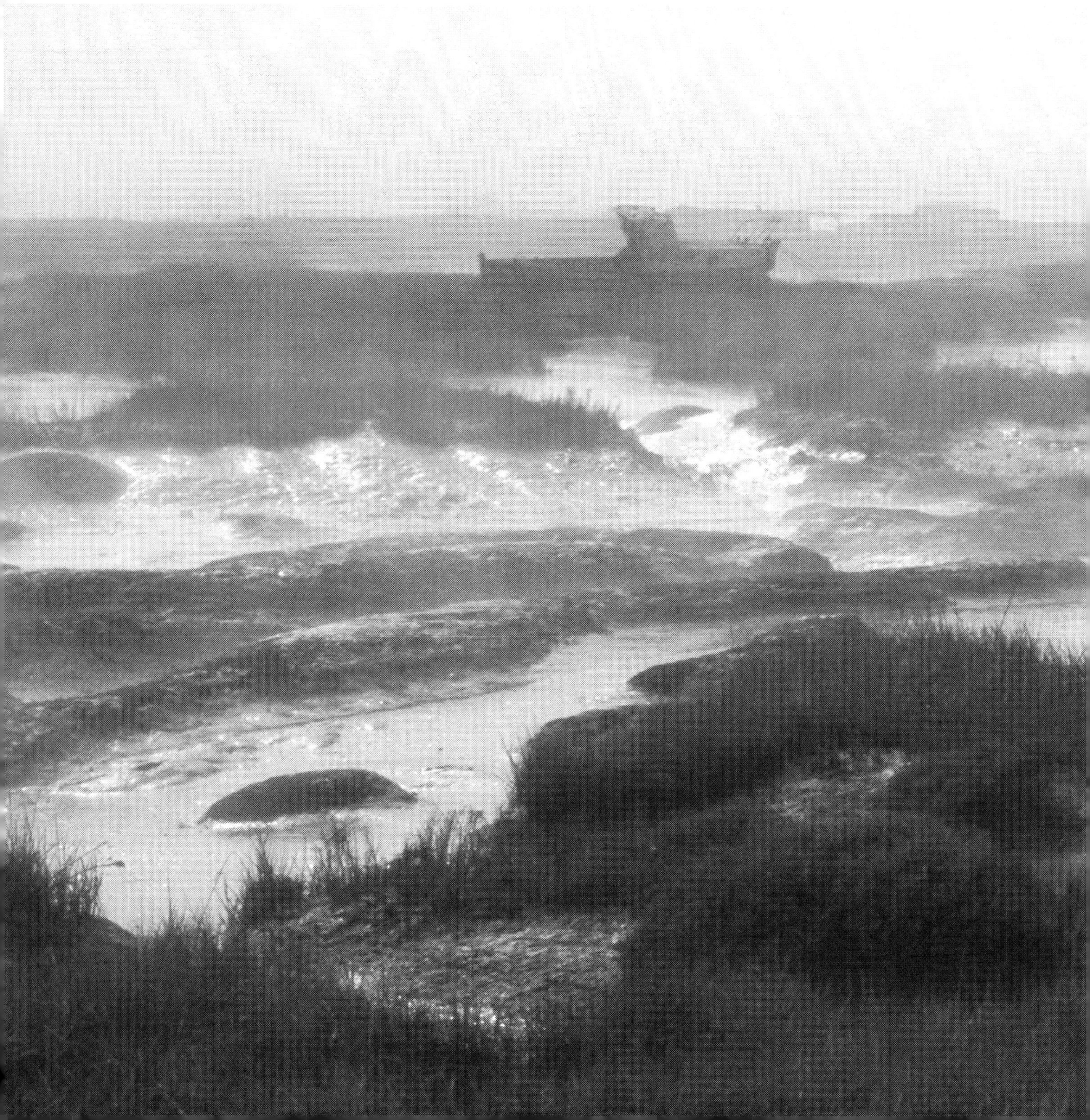

## SEA ASTERS AT DAWN

This is not the sun - surely:
red, like a sudden wound, it rises
where the fog becomes a bruise across the sea.

The geese are not quite geese:
guardians of daylight's open gate
their gutturals are dog-like as they bark
    in black battalions.

The sphere, the blood, the corpuscle, this globe
            - is now a gash -
an injury, a scar without a fight, where all is peace.

How strange the contradictions of the dawn
as night's preoccupations are erased
by visions such as this
across the flats

where saltings, creeks and gullies
are transformed by light's slow treatment.

All is recuperation as the crows
caw in such a way that their contempt is disregarded
and even the brents that barked in disarray
are softened by the sunlight turning gold
    and dawn's redemption.

The asters in October, just a floss
that's gilded by the promise of Saint Luke
and in this still, remedial contusion,
all thoughts of frost and snow are not of loss -
        more like a bandage.

ML

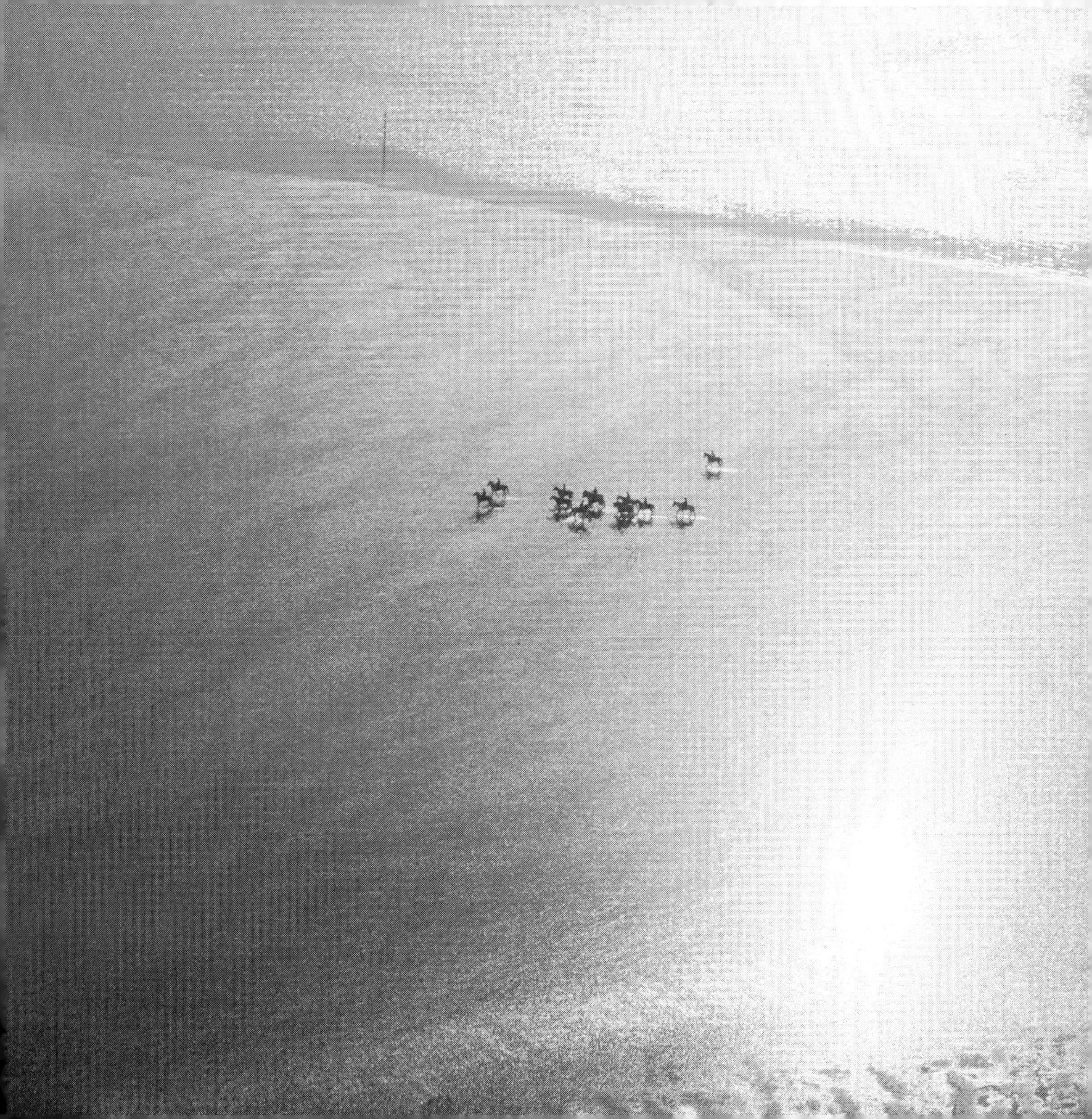

## FLIGHT

Once in my eagle days
I flew over Maplin,
Wide as a desert
Stretched shimmering sand.

Masters of never-land,
Loose-reined and joyous,
Earthbound the riders
Galloped the strand.

Free in their element
Flocks of white sea birds,
Wheeling and tumbling –
Kings of the air.

Who was the winner,
Sea birds or riders
Or I, the dreamer,
Above them, aware…?

RH

## MAY THE FIFTH

The arrival of the swifts - For days
I've watched,
    nothing;
And yet here they are,
Five on the evening air
Curved into substance
By the thought of summer.

Cuneiform on blue papyrus -
Fluent with contrast;
All night they'll fly -
Ink to the sky's ink,
Lost to the liquid
Of the leaching stars.

    Tomorrow,
When the flowers wake -
When the words of fragrance
Climb on the voices
Of the warming earth;
  They'll underline
The languages they make -
Screech over paper,
Like a nib that scratches.

ML

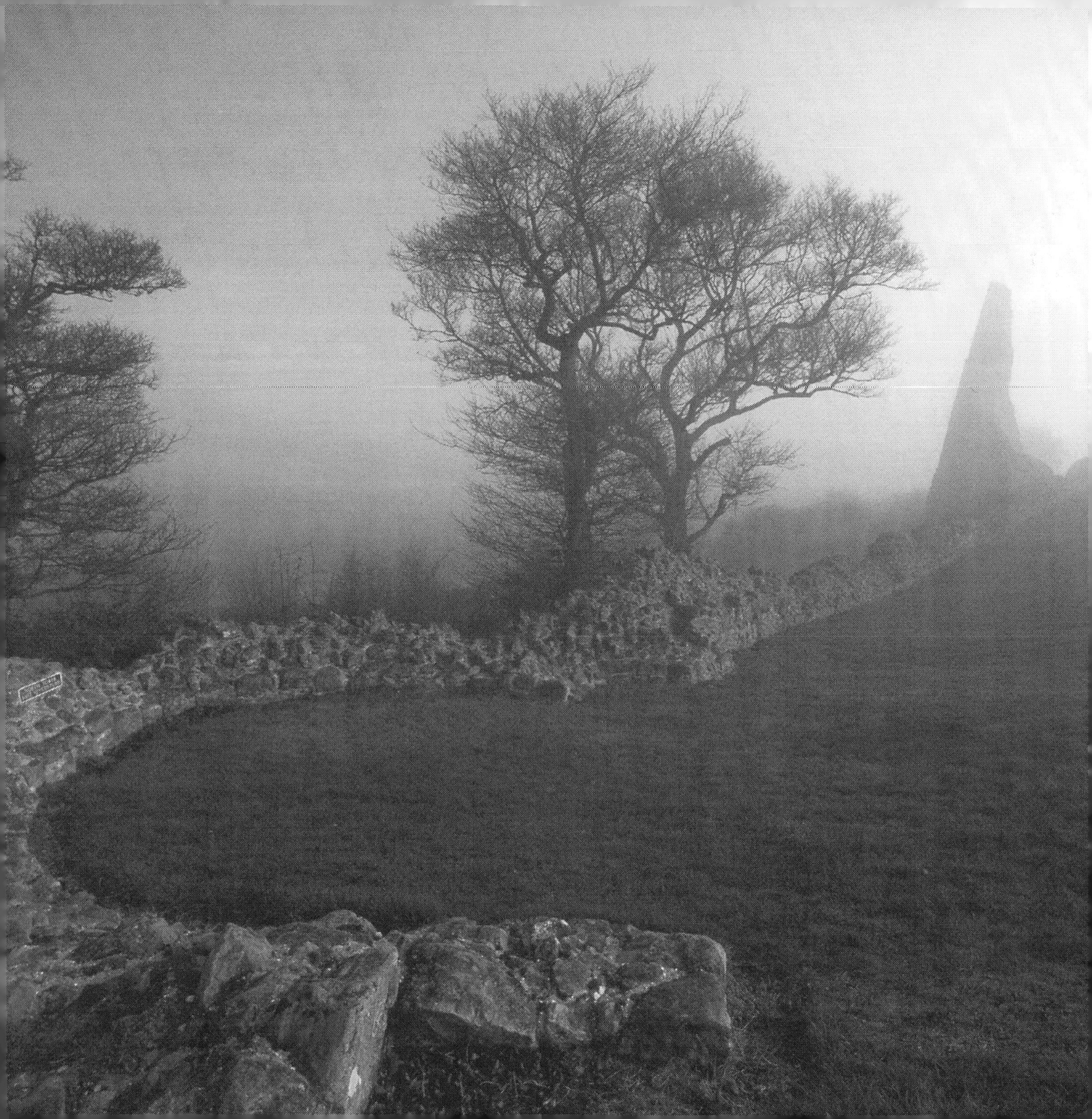

## GOOSEBERRY FAYRE

Gooseberry Pie!
Gooseberry Pie!
Who will buy
My Gooseberry Pie?

Gooseberry filling with pastry on top,
Less than a shilling, we eat 'til we pop.
Round dish or square shape, in Hadleigh each year
Come all ye folks to ye Gooseberry Fayre!

Gooseberry Pie!
Gooseberry Pie!
Who will buy
My Gooseberry Pie?

Come to the castle and come to the Downs,
Cycle along with a smile, not with frowns.
Sporting Olympics on bumpy terrain,
Down on the marshes they're coming by train.

Gooseberry Pie!
Gooseberry Pie!
Who will buy
My Gooseberry Pie?

Come to St James the Less not the Most,
Come say a prayer, we need it the most.
Look for the Cunning Man Murrell with care:-
Come all ye folks to ye Gooseberry Fayre!

Gooseberry Poi!
Gooseberry Poi!
Who will boy
My Gooseberry Poi?

RH

## HADLEIGH IN NOVEMBER

Landscape retreats into nothing but distance.
Cobwebs hang heavy with dew.
Crystal-clear droplets like beads on a necklet.
Fog shrouds the castle from view.

Pigeon at rest in its oak tree perch morning,
Treetops nod gently, like reeds.
Muted the drone of a riverboat's warning.
Sound, like the ebb tide, recedes.

Rattling, a ghost train rolls by on the marshes.
Ghost ships pass close to the shore.
Calves, half-asleep, graze the Downs' Sally Army.
Kings ride in splendour of yore.

Just for a moment the retinue lingers.
Queens find their home of a kind.
Over your spine travel icy-damp fingers.
Footsteps – or hooves – in the mind?

RH

## SIRENS – THAMES ESTUARY

Looking out across the sandbanks and the ooze
to where Tewkes Creek and Hadleigh's shallow Ray
meander through their serpentine constraints
towards the width of this wide estuary
my mind like all the tides and all the days
that I've sat here and watched the distant sea
is fathomed by the ebb and then the flow
of memory and those mean water springs
when anchored and afloat in Neptune's sway
we fished October's Middle Grounds for cod
        and channel whiting.

And when the fog, mysterious and grey,
appeared as if from nowhere to restrain all thought and vision
I felt as though estranged from this cold world
with but the call of curlews and the gulls
to underline existence and explain
            the living breath.

The throb of some great diesel driven piston
described the unseen image of a ship
too close to us, just off the starboard bow, and getting closer
and then the fear of all the drowning dark
augmented by the fog horn's mournful voice
reminded us that myth still manifests
as Charybdis and Scylla did their best
to wreck our youthful spirits, thus becalmed,
with thoughts that plumbed as deeply as the depths
        of truth and meaning.

ML

## HALLOWEEN AT HADLEIGH CASTLE

Let us celebrate at the Midnight hour
On the shivering hill by the castle tower,
Where the night is black and the stones are cold
And many a tale still waits to be told…

Of the shadows dark that are flitting past,
Of the eerie sounds and the sudden blast
When a jealous wind moves the cobwebs bleak
While the frightened souls their come-uppance seek.

Let us celebrate where the wizard roamed,
The Grey Lady waits and the smugglers moaned.
The Grey Lady slaps you across your face
As you hurry home to a safer place.

And your skin feels cold and your blood will curdle
When the Wizard passes aloft on his hurdle.
Let us celebrate at the Midnight hour
Ere a moonbeam reaches the castle tower…

RH

## DOPPELGANGER

The crow with his eyes
like midnight, void of stars -
  connects with mine

and the sun with its faceless face of Halloween
blind to the ghosted moment and the veil
    that parts
revealing what we would not see
  is an orange glow.

Supposing now as grass frost slowly bleeds
and your dawning breath that rises and accedes
  to the misted light

was really a formless spectre
   - not a dream -
  that is manifesting.

The crow with his midnight eyes up in the oak
where tarnished gold is nipped and then released
   by icy fingers

knows without the knowingness of creeds
that the daylight's smoke and mirrors

- our beliefs -

like the leaves
that float and fall
or the breath that

- lingers -

are nothing more
than auguries or omens -
just walking doubles.

ML

## HEYBRIDGE EVENING

To the west the brimming shallows
Reed-rimmed, bracken, man-made ponds.
Chirping avocets, like swallows
Diving low across the fronds.

Diving where the sun is drowning
Milk and cream and lilac bright,
Orange dripping its reflection
Ere the stars present the night.

Upwards to the dying glory
Maldon's dainty steeple points –
From the darkening land of story
Human sentiment anoints.

Once the sluggish waters ploughing,
Barges, black in reverie –
Shallow-drafted, tides allowing –
Huddle at the ancient quay.

Stands the heron, silent, watching.
On this April evening's end.
Gentle swans, like lovers, touching,
Glide to where the shadows blend.

Over, from the hawthorn thicket,
Close the sturdy, stagnant lock
Calls a Cuckoo, sly and wicked,
Where the pride of Heybridge dock.

Tinkering, the week-end sailor
On his smart appointed craft,
As the burning sky grows paler,
Preens a little, fore and aft.

Snug the 'Jolly Sailor' beckons,
Lanterns lure 'The Old Ship' –
"Let's ashore, old mate, Oi reckons,
While we dream another trip."

To the east, where Panta's river
Circles Northey's broken isles –
Are they ghosts that make me shiver?
Dying men? Or seagulls' cries?

RH

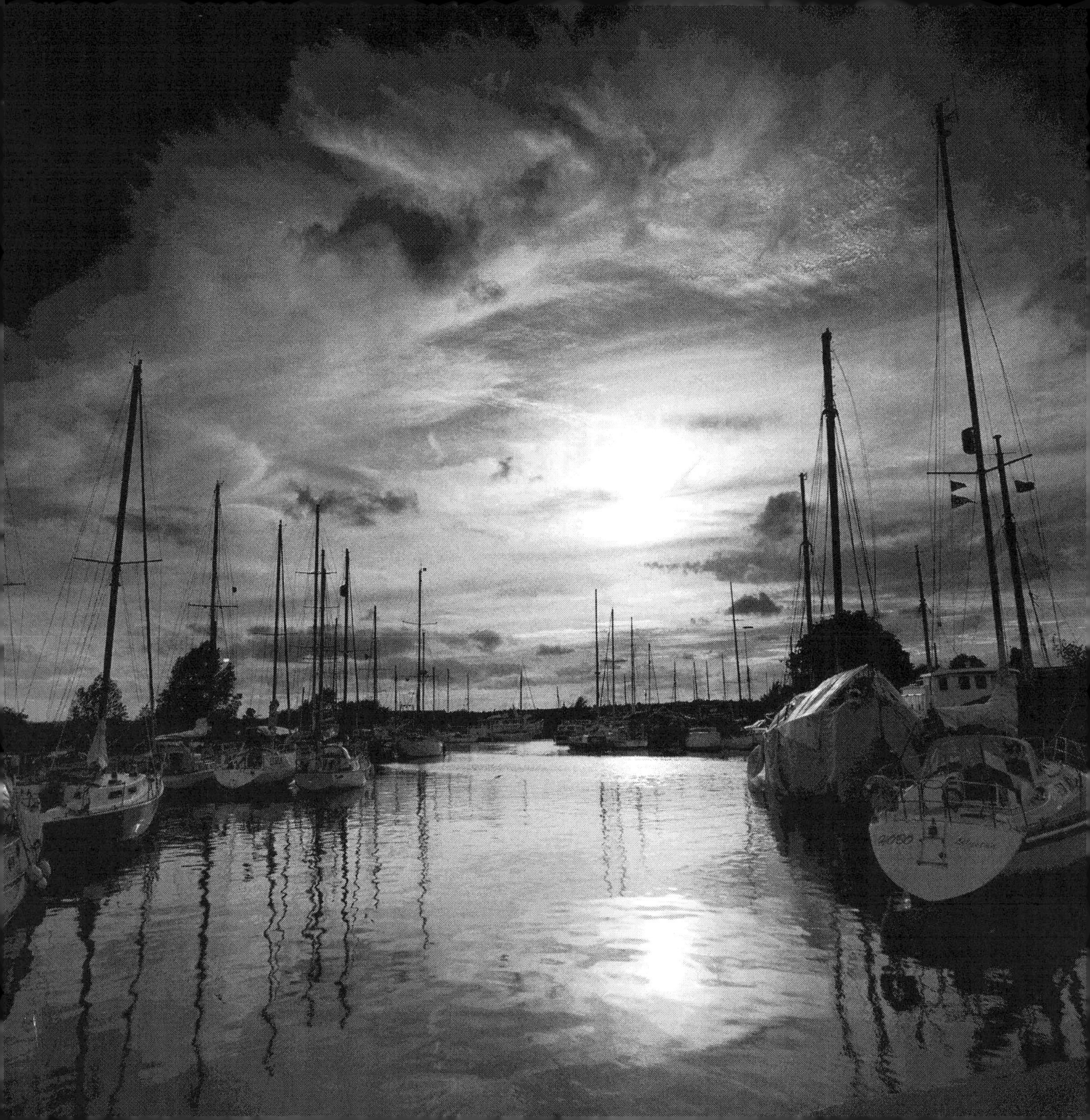

## BLACKWATER ESTUARY

There are views and there are visions. Across
the fields from here, the low hills and the tree-
lined ridges, there appears a world awash

with creeks and islands. A silvered world
of ooze and endless saltings where egrets
walk on stilts and curlew call and every pearl

is housed within its oyster. What is the cost
of visions such as these, where every breeze
is seasoned by the sun and I am lost

to language - close to love? A swan unfurls
its wings. A bell-beat sounds. And my regrets
are nothing, are undone, by time's deferral.

A sprit'sle's ochre sails attain the sea
but my heart's keel: lies here - amongst the cockles.

ML

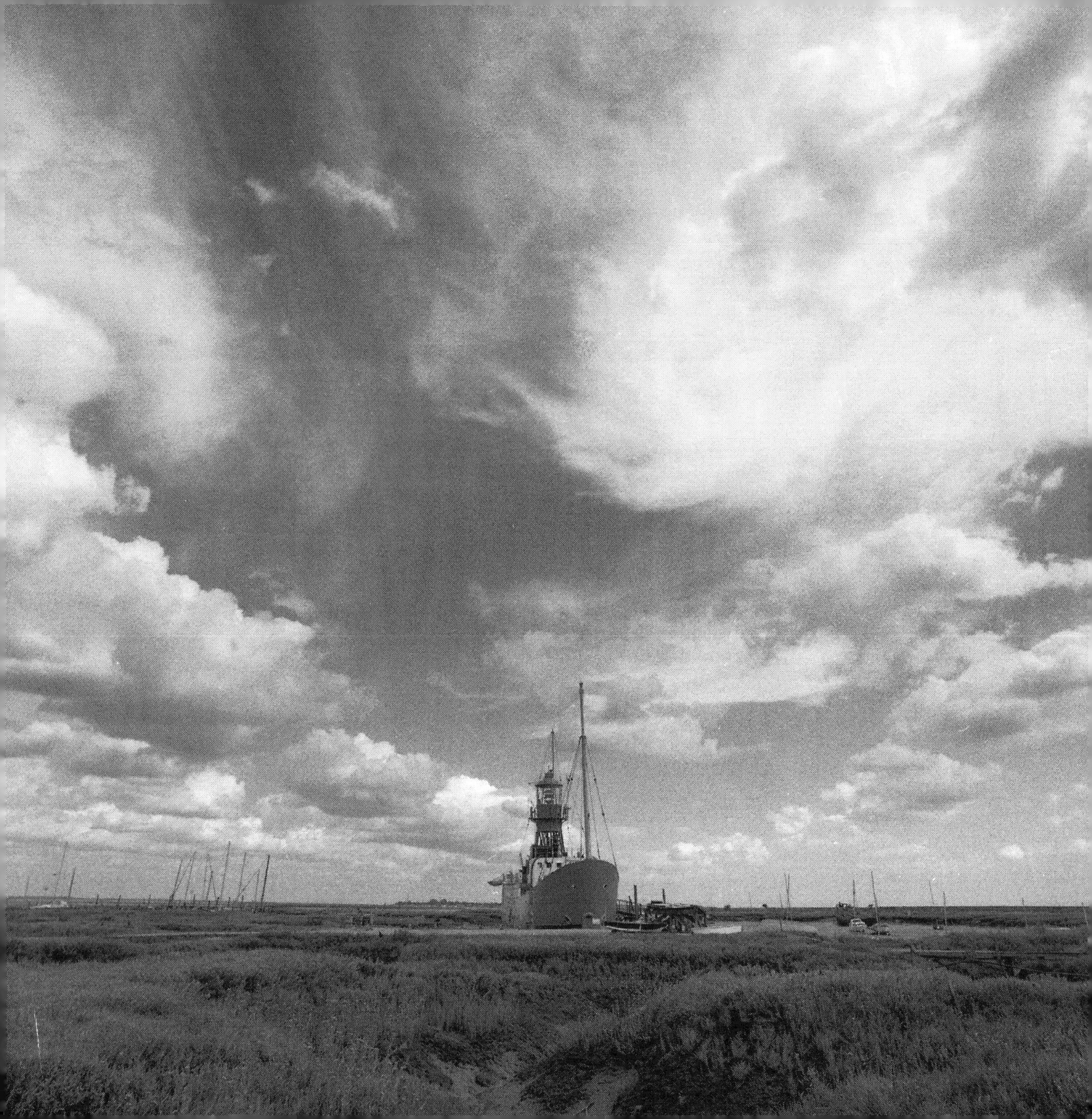

## OCTOBER STORM

The plough has turned the red-brown sod to autumn,
Cool air strikes low across the new-ridged earth.
Flocks of bright seagulls shimmer as they tumble
And soar the blue-black sky in bursts of mirth.

Now Thunor rants and throws his shiny hammer.
The heavens clash and cry a myriad tears.
What happened to the golden days of summer?
How quickly turned the portents into fears…

At Corringham, the ever belching towers,
Their horizontal fumes sucked from their mouths,
Rake pregnant clouds throughout the blustering hours.
Where beauty withers, no tomorrow grows.

Yet beauty wins and blooms among the thunder.
One sacred finger mopish darkness shames –
One sunbeam tears the bloated clouds asunder
And liquid silver shimmers on the Thames…

RH

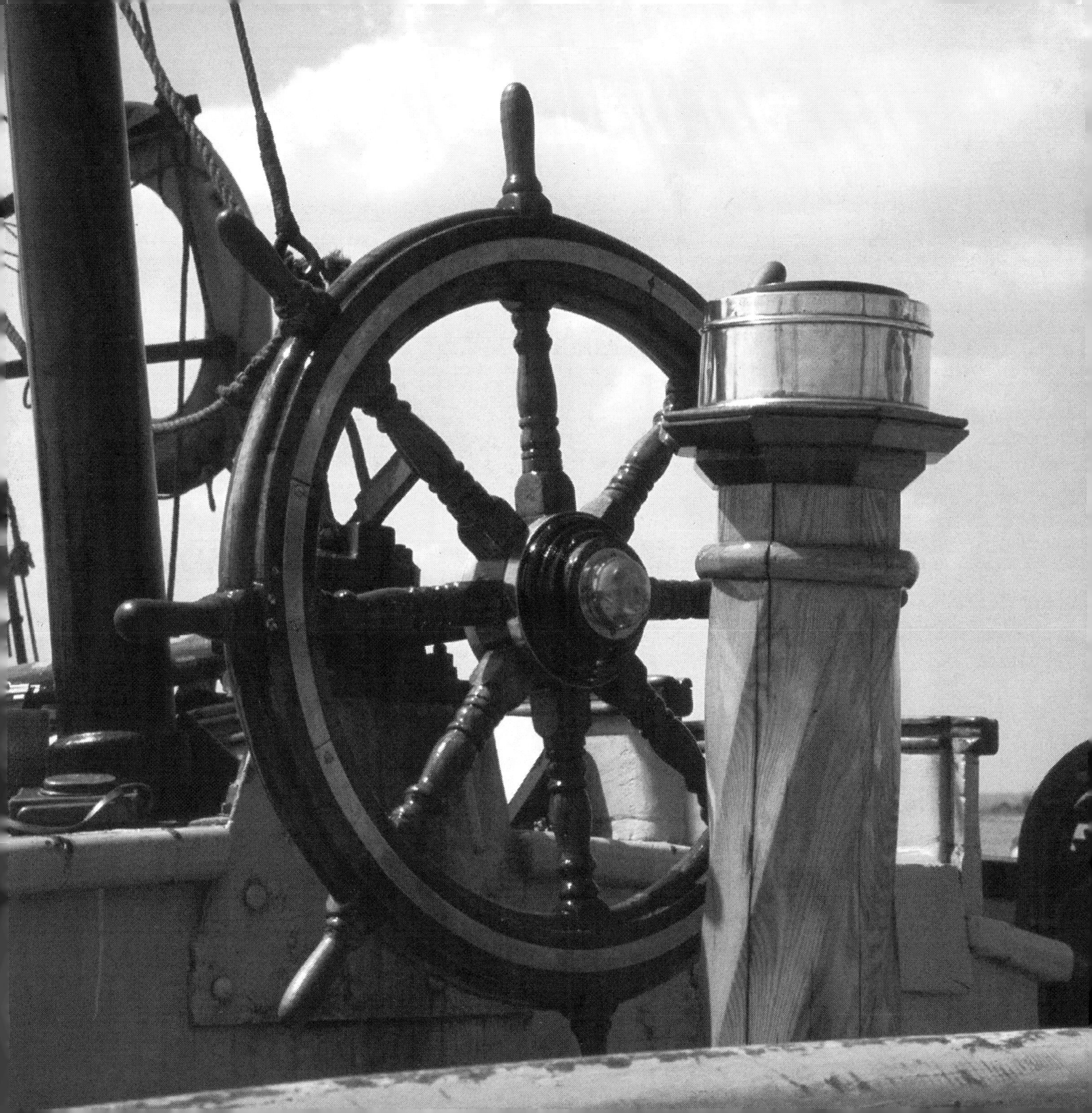

## NORTH SEA PASSAGE

Out here, between Holland, perhaps Norfolk,
Suffolk or Essex, it's far from calm.

The wind, north, northwest, force eight or nine,
with a swell to match, tests the stability of the ship
    and its passengers.

The sea shudders under the hull, investigates the bows,
surmounts them like a racehorse over hurdles
then floods the deck, possessively.

Something thrums amongst the rigging - the superstructure:
a siren singing an ancient song; a lamentation.

At all points of the stormy compass
there is nothing to observe except the sea:
no chart, no bearings, nothing for the sense of where we are -

only greyness, rain at a slant, or horizontal;
the occasional gull or gannet blown awry -
      like an albatross.

ML

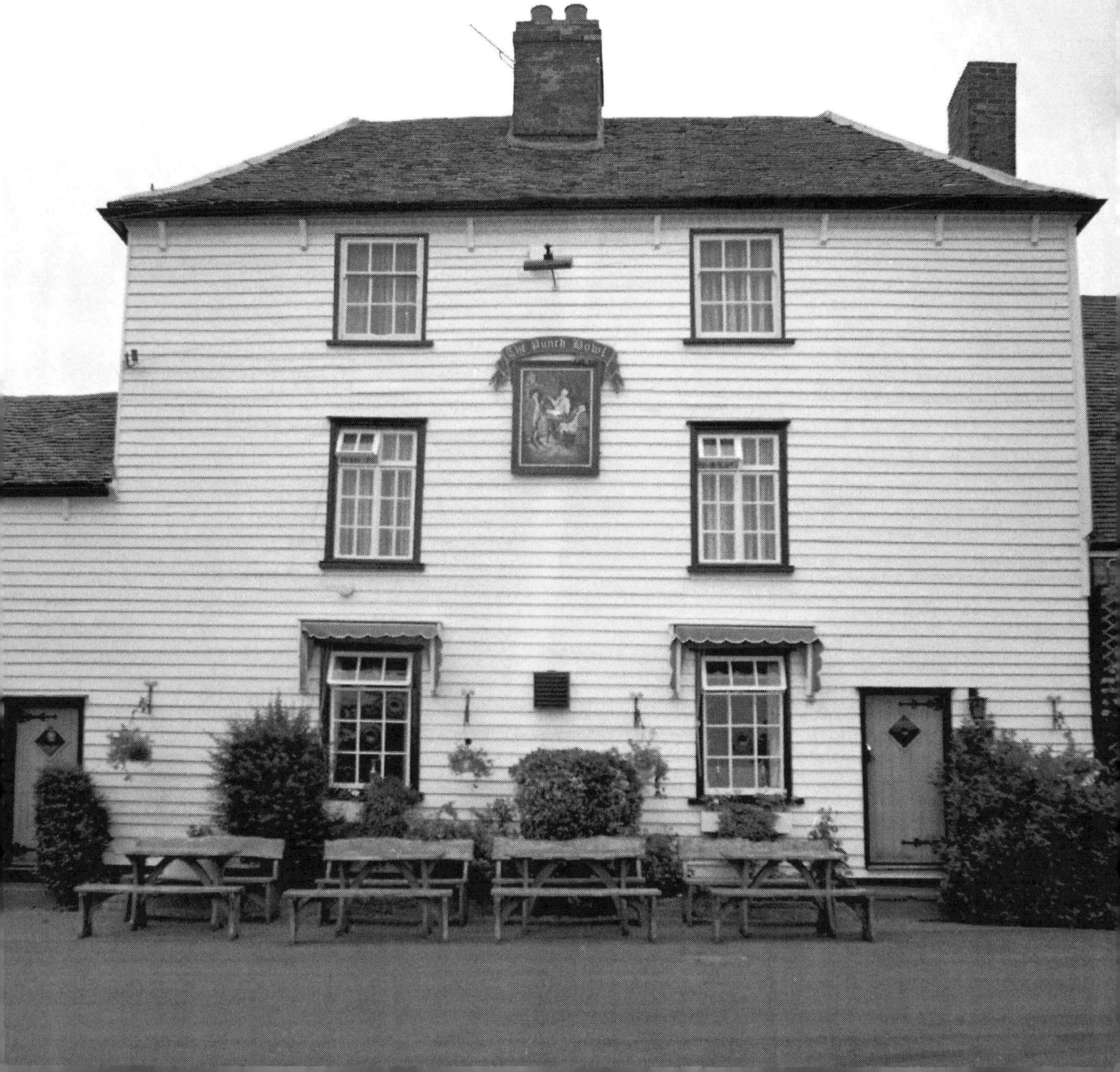

## PAGLESHAM SUMMER

A beetle scuttles to and fro
On business only beetles know –
And over at the tidal creek
Some squabbling seagulls scratch and shriek.

A pheasant breaks with noisy wings,
Then heads for home and better things –
Not so the heron, who, with stealth
Seeks of the muddy briny's wealth.

Where moth and butterfly cavort
At night the quiet owl makes sport
And leaves her calling card behind.
Regurgitated pellets find...

A bumbling bee, his hackles swollen
Alights, delights, bedecked with pollen.
Assist the male and female thing
And joy to other flowers bring.

A hare stops on his favourite trail,
Then shakes a leg and shows his tail.
Slow down, relax, don't give a damn.
The world's at peace at Paglesham.

RH

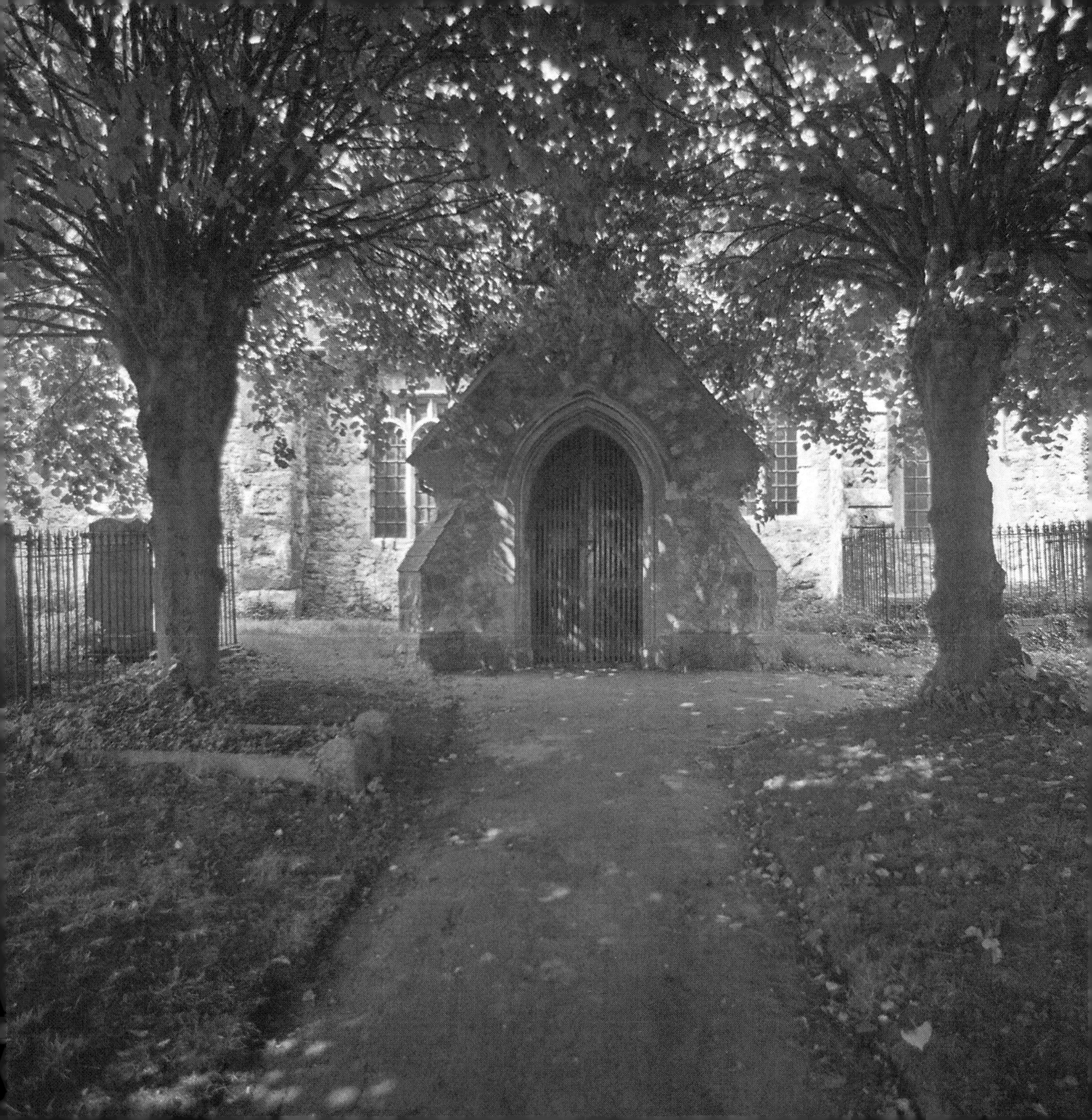

**SAND MARTINS**
(Evening Roost - Paglesham)

There were sand martins:
        just a few -
the other year they settled here in thousands
and no-one knew exactly whence they came.

Speculation: chooses what it will -
sandpits in Essex, Suffolk, or Norfolk;
the steep-sided banks of our Anglian rivers.

They had more sand to come -
their sub-Saharan winters drew them on
towards the sun and other warming instincts.

The evening roost expanded:
the wires could not hold them -
strange staves - strange notations.

The music summer makes can overcome -
    dirges, laments, threnodies,
all the valedictions and the strains
        of mournful cellos.

    Thousands, thousands,
beating their wings against the harvest moon:
that massive, molten, amber-full illusion
resounding: in the owl-light - like a drum.

ML

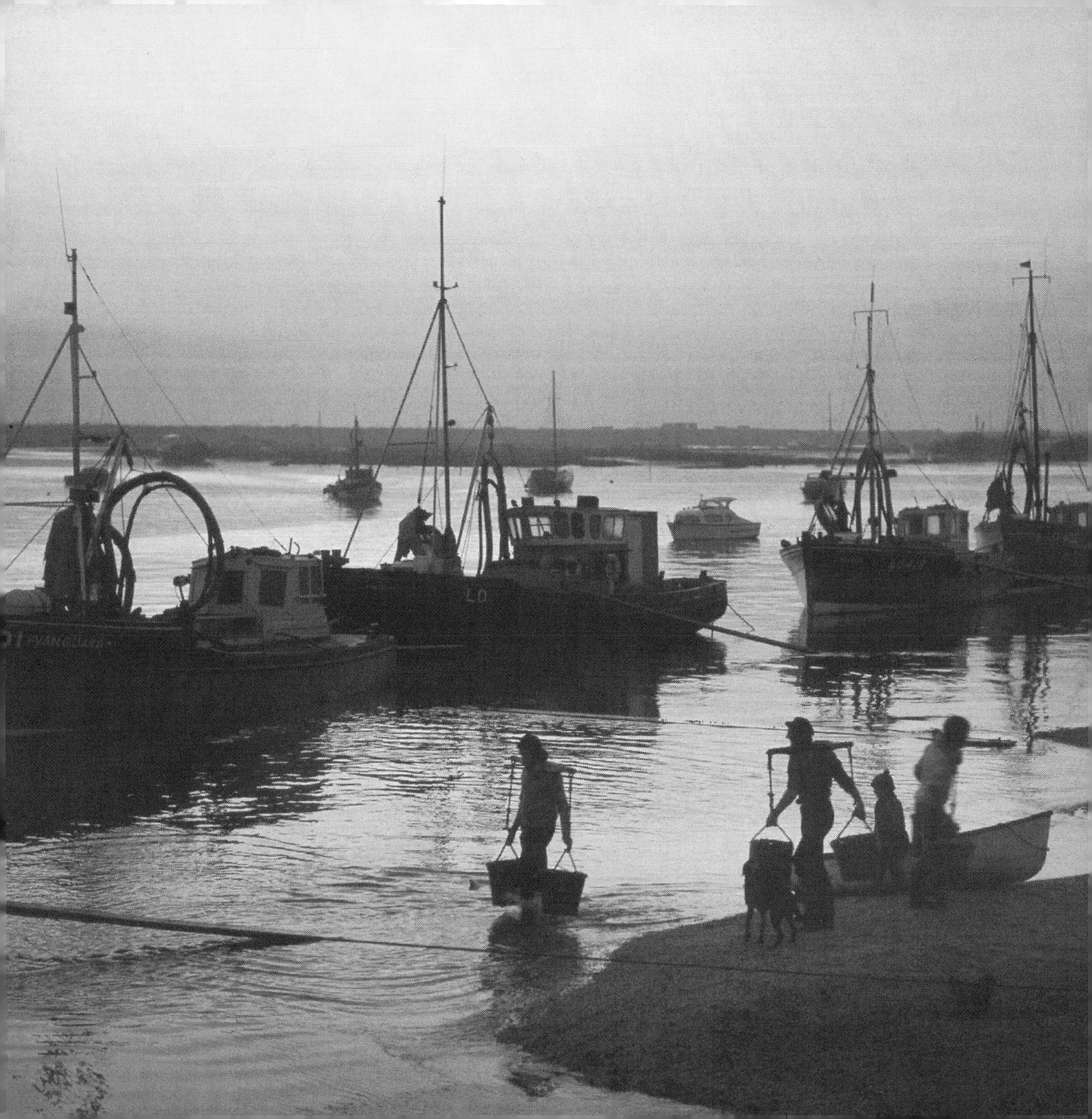

## SONG OF LEIGH

From way above the cockling trips
St. Clement's guides the little ships
That scour the Thames and suck and seek
Come rain or shine in Smugglers' Creek.

In finger licking cockle-sheds
Arrives the fruit of oyster beds,
While all the time our nostrils thrill
To odours only Leigh can fill.

The Thames rolls by, one sits and chats
Next tree-less Two-Tree-Island's flats,
To keep our spirits well afloat
With chasers at the Peterboat.

I like to be,
Delightedly,
In cobbly, wobbly Leigh-on-Sea.

RH

## UNLOADING COCKLES
(Leigh-on-Sea)

The cockle fleet uplifts the artist's thumb
and frames itself in old-world atmospherics.

The sun loads light across the creek
and girls with skin like umber
tease their impressions in a swirl of pastel.

We read the signs that vie for evocation:
Peter Boat and Smack
Old Ship and Crooked Billet.

Along the streets and cobble-dinted lanes
shadows from houses
angle like easels in a clash of contrast.

The sea beyond
scumbles the skyline into blue opaquely –
blurs into billows of diminished ochre.

A man with a heavy yoke
changes perspective, like a print that's faded –
carries the burden of intense nostalgia.

ML

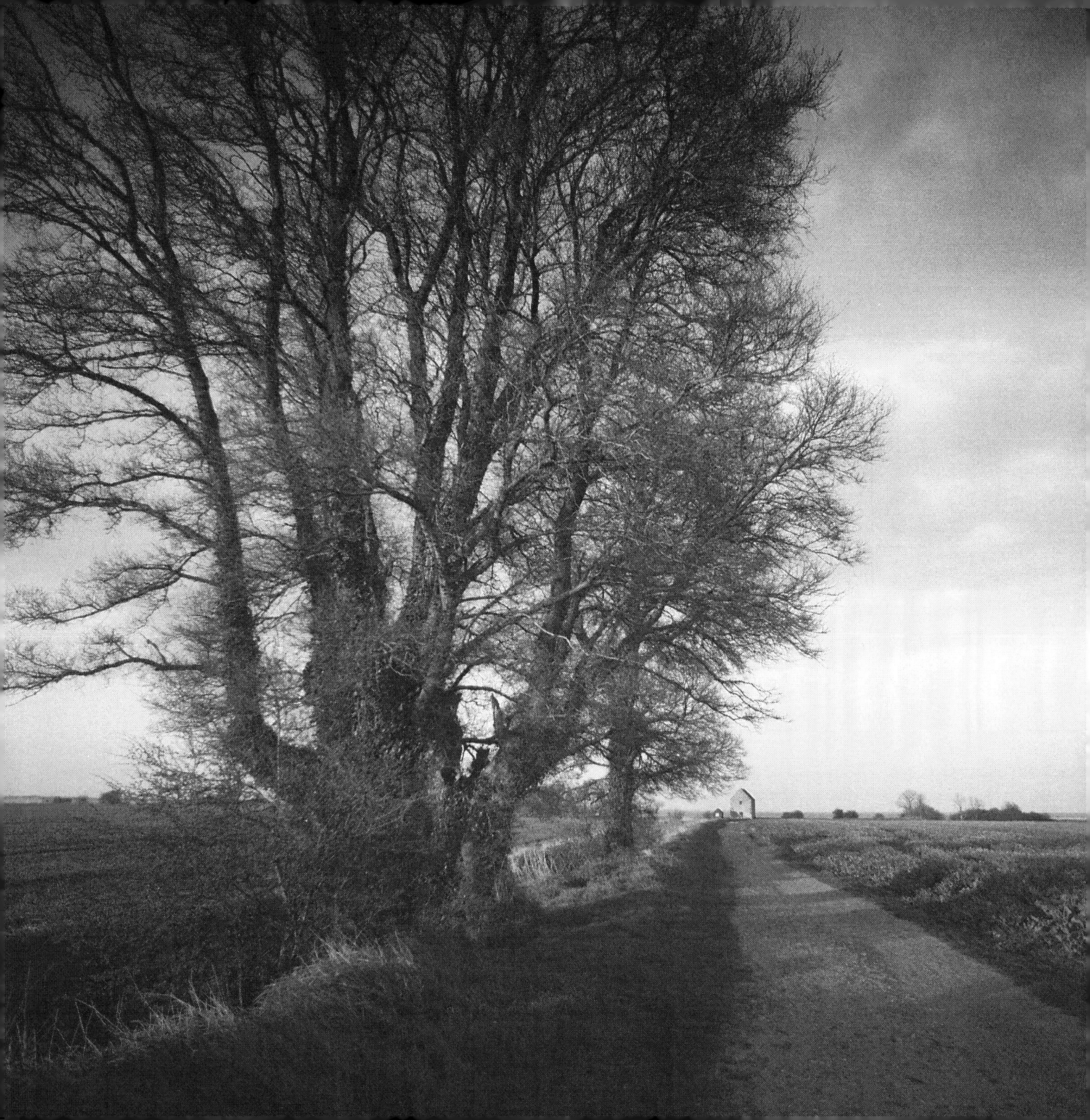

## THE POACHER ON THE NESS

He sat alone in the dead of night
With his trusty gun resting by his side –
For his deeds he couldn't care less.
And moonlight brightened the eerie scene.
Where the seawall rises he can't be seen,
On the still expanse of the Ness.

But as he surveyed the reeded pond,
The brackish water, the sea beyond,
The night's kill safe in his sack,
The poacher froze, in his heart aware
Of a loathsome presence that fixed its stare
At the central point of his back.

Call it intuition or what you will,
But he grabbed his gun and he turned, quite still,
Controlled and determined and mean –
For there, above him on higher ground
A ghastly spectre, a hoary hound
Picked out by the moon's silv'ry sheen.

It stood shoulder high and it seemed to grow,
Its fangs bared white and its eyes aglow –
Yet his cool resolve fought for control.
And the trigger jammed and there was no sound.
Immovably eyed him the slobbering hound,
Its eyes burning right to his soul.

The poacher panicked, he felt absurd.
Yet he remembered his father's word:
"Don't show any fear to Black Shuck!
Don't turn your back on old Odin's hound.
If you want to stay breathing above the ground
Don't turn your back on Black Shuck!"

He ignored those words as he dropped his gun
And he turned on his heels and he ran and ran,
Expecting its grizzly attack.
As he turned to be sure in his headlong flight
The creature kept following stride for stride
To the very door of his shack.

The following morning, to prove his worth,
He retraced his steps – in the dew-fresh earth
His tracks could be easily found.
He picked up his gun as it lay there still,
But nowhere a sign of his bloody kill –
NOR THE PAW PRINTS OF A HOUND!

RH

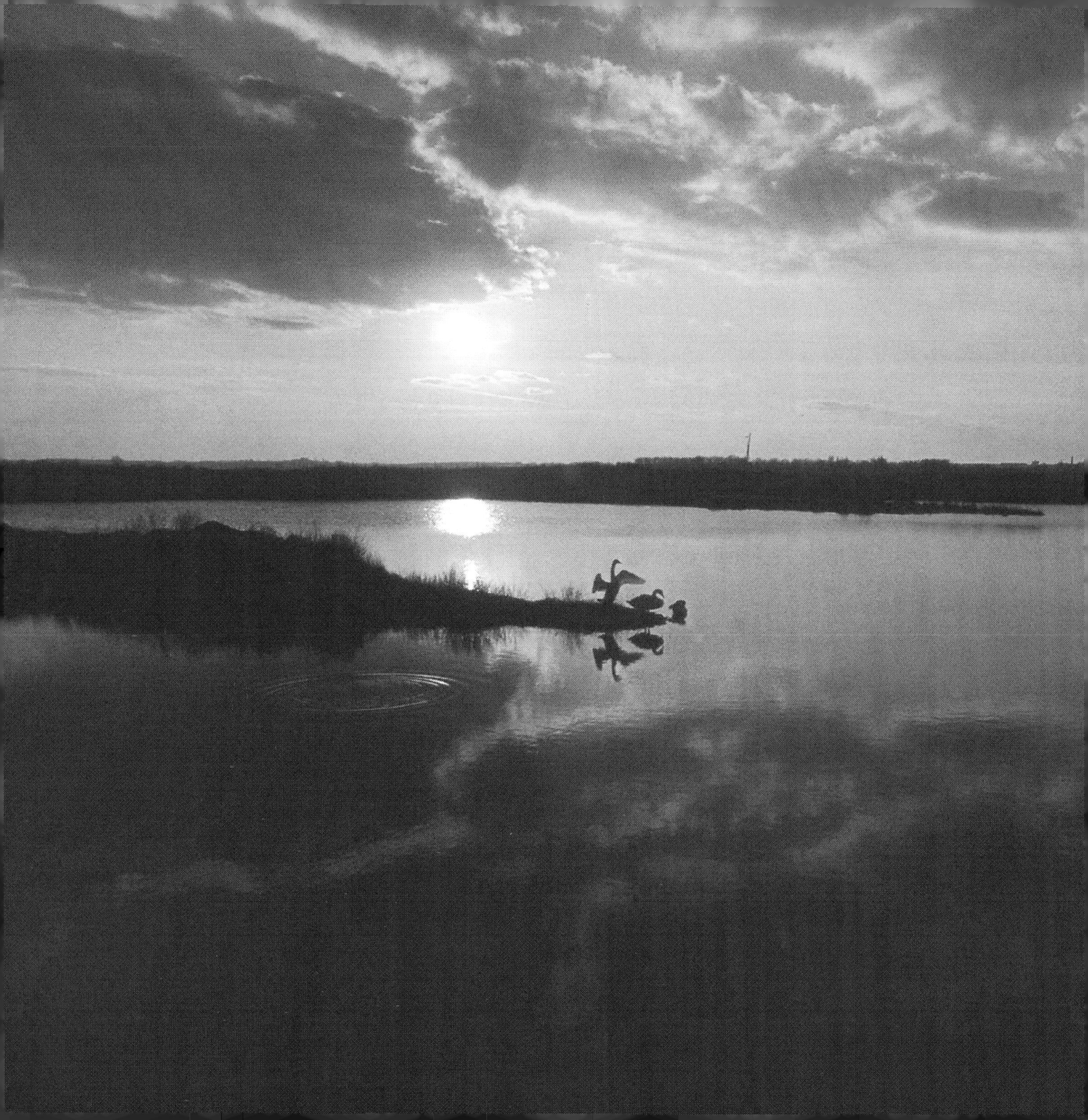

## THE FALCONER

Ulting Church River Chelmer

It could have been any age:
The man with a buzzard on his arm -
The church and the river.

He could have been a knight
    or a prince -
Chasing the hare, the rabbit.

The buzzard came to his whistle
    like a dog:
Flew from the tree -
Greeted his arm with talons.

The excitements are the same -
Though tinged with guilt.

I wanted to see the quarry
    and the kill:
The grace at wing, the aerobatics.

I wanted to see the hare across the fields:
The twist and turn of feather over fur -
    the skill surviving.

ML

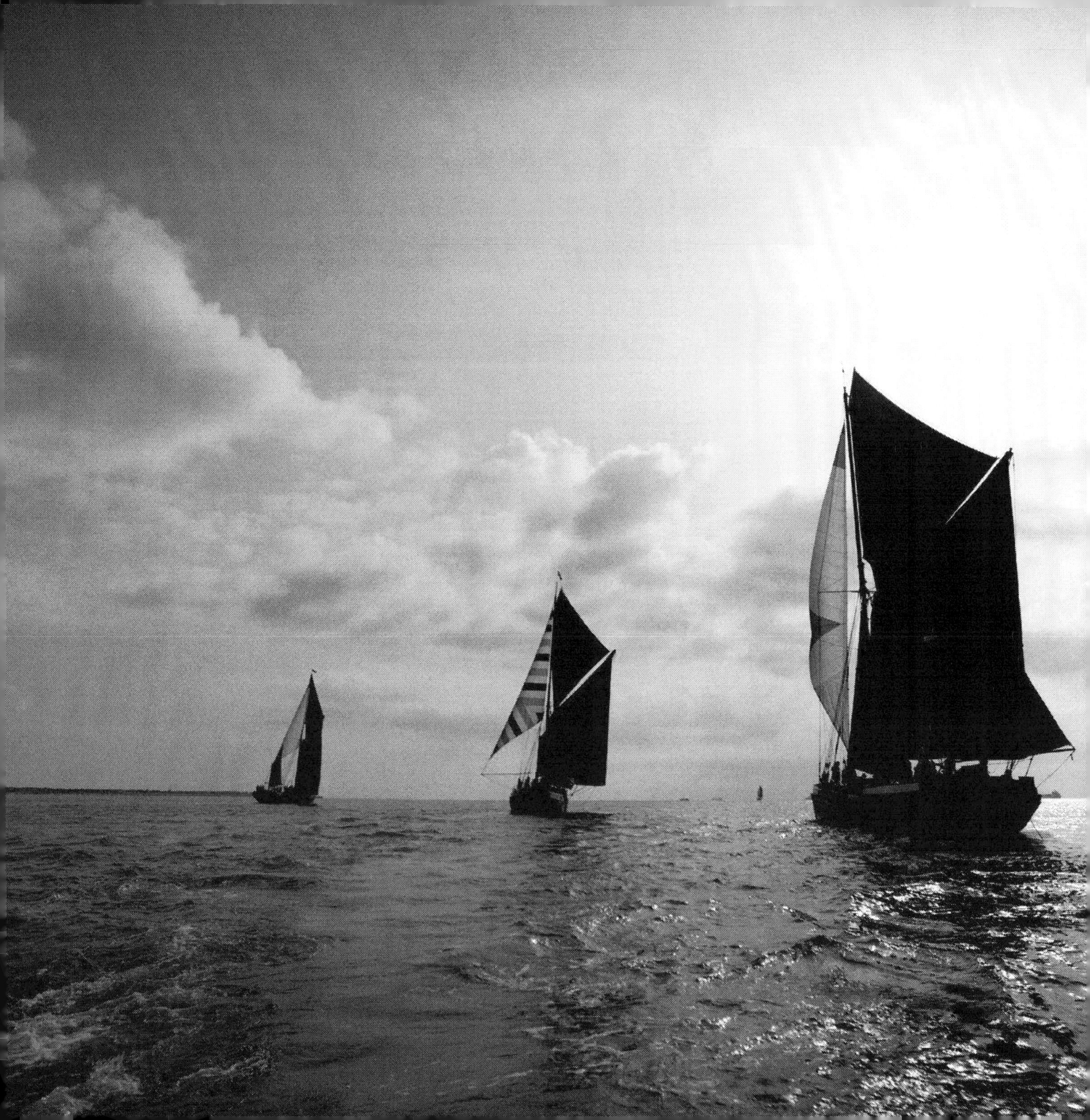

**THE SILENT FLEET**

When night falls on the ancient coast
And stars abound, the sparkling host
Reflect in every ripple small,
The night owl hoots its eerie call
And quietness cloaks all,

Then rises proud a silent fleet
Of spectres from the muddy deep.
And all the ships that ever sunk
Or rotted on a muddy bank
Reclaim their former rank

As ghostly shadows. Floating free,
The lichen hulks take to the sea.
And masts appear where pennants flew.
From Davie's Locker climbs the crew,
And sails unfurl anew.

And black, barge black, the spritsails glide
From friendly quays on wind and tide,
From busy Harwich to the Nore,
From all around the sleeping shore
Collect the silent corps.

But none who sleep will ever see
The little ships take to the sea
And travel to a foreign strand
To pluck the soldiers from the sand
As brothers, hand in hand…

RH

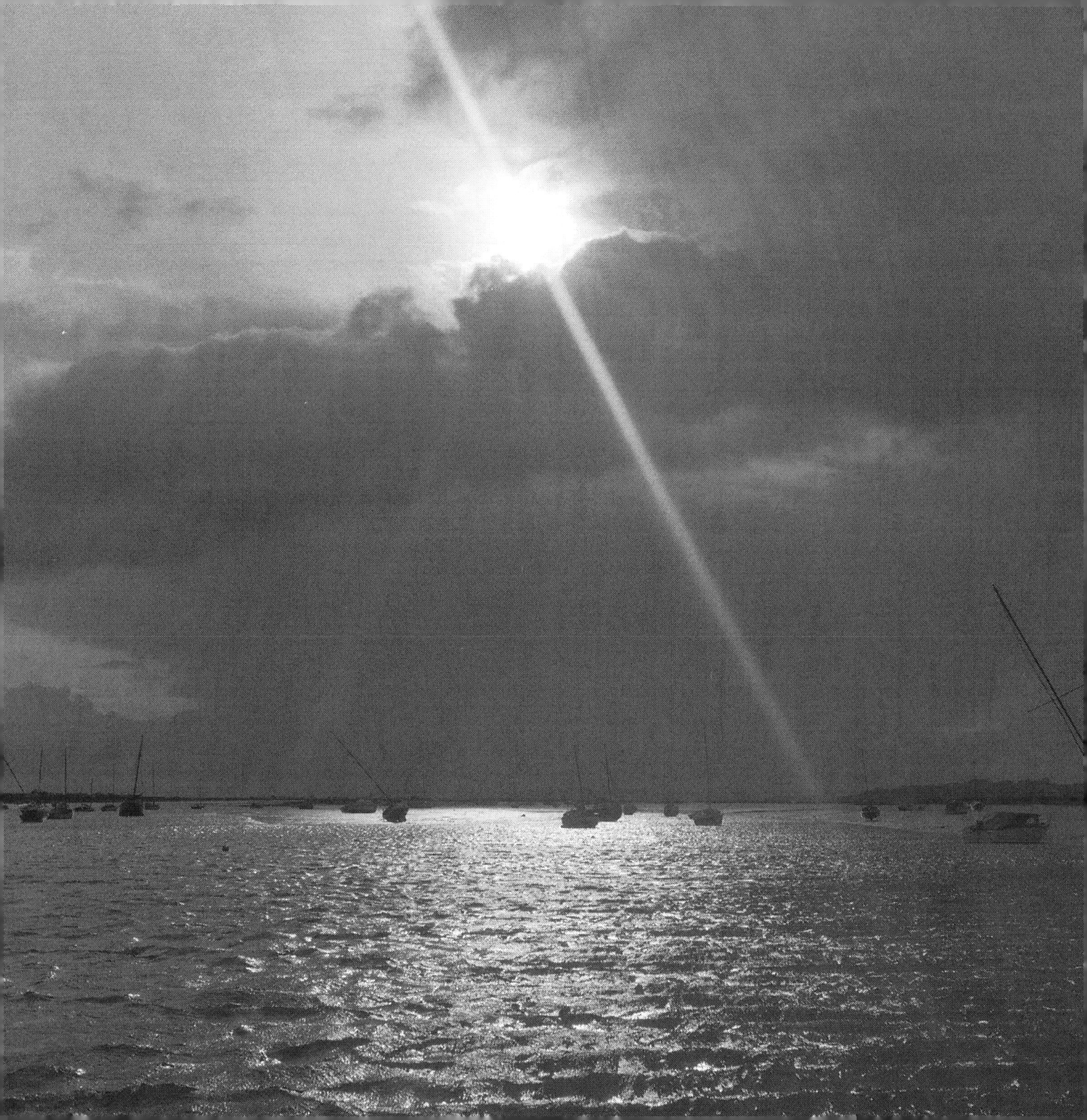

## SEASCAPE IN NOVEMBER

My vehicle is buffeted by the wind:
here in the carpark on Mersea Island facing west
where the tide lapping at the level of the land is as grey as
the sky's inclemency.

Yachts – moored or at anchor – ride the increasing whiteness
of the waves, like horses over Beecher's Brook
only to slam and flounder helplessly on the other side.

Memories of men who dredged for oysters
and lived out their J Class lives under the ensign
with pride and a sense of superior purpose
are forgotten now as children freed at last
from digital enslavement
dangle their bacon fat and rind for the green
and bubbling surprise of astounded shore crabs.

Migratory birds: passerines, waders and wildfowl
ignore the shifting borders that infiltrate our minds
and the annuls of history to settle down
across the thoughtless saltings and the creeks
to feed and further instinct and survival.

The rain comes on and slants across the Strood
as I regain the mainland's other side
where legions marched and Boudicca defied all Roman Rule
as far as distant London

and I who've lived with Essex as my guide
beneath the seaxe of this old Saxon Kingdom
inscribe these words despairing of all tribes
and thank the gods of lavender and purslane
for all the cold-indifference of their eyes
and what they've seen.

ML

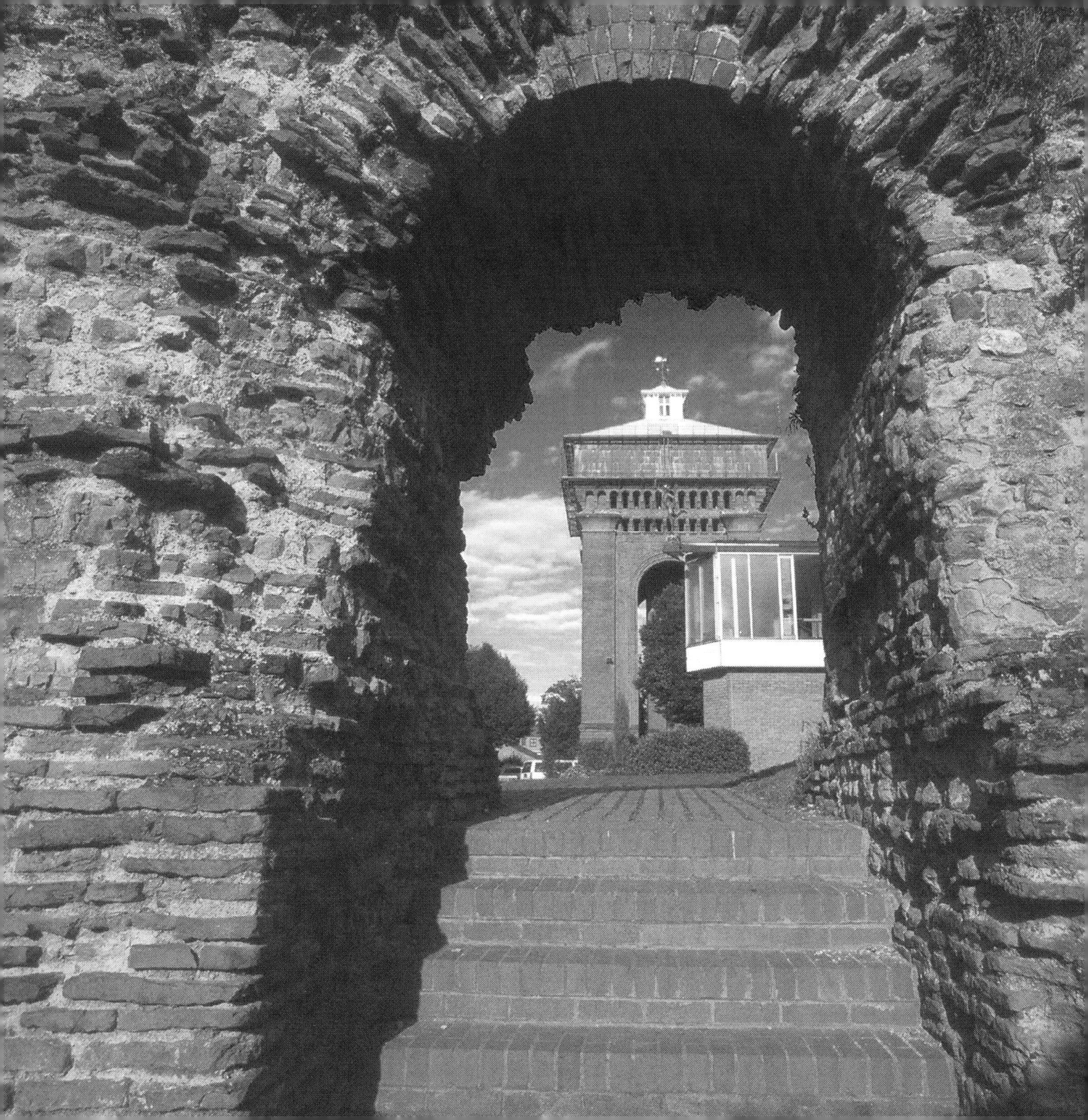

## COLCHESTER

I drove among the daffodils to Colchester this day,
With golden heads anodding, they bade this stranger stay.

I stood in Claudius' temple and ducked below its walls,
I listened to Old English and warlike Latin calls.

I walked among Iceni and Romans in my mind,
All in a Norman castle among my fellow kind.

I lived the siege of roundheads and suffered with their kin.
Reduced to eating horses, shut gates kept us within,

When brother fought with brother and father fought with son,
The commoners v. kingship, the King v. common man.

The bullet holes still pepper the inn and tell the plight,
When many a weeping mother cursed king and folk alike.

I heard the shots that fired, on Parliament's behest.
Upon the town's surrender, they tore the loyal chests.

I drove among the daffodils to Colchester this day,
With golden heads a-nodding, they bade me on my way.

RH

## A DAFFODIL IN DECEMBER

Say what you like about the world
but I am part of everything I've known
and the sentiment's reciprocal.

When it rains I weep for the showers in spring
and all the sunlit daffodils that cling -
like the bleating lambs.

Even the roar of lions through the trees
inspired me to revel in my breath
and listen to the breathing of a sky
that rang the weather's changes and the knell
of all that's frozen.

And when the sun spoke loudly without words
and climbed above the curdled cumuli
into the solemn apogee of blue
and boundless heat

where glacial the clouds on high belied
analogies of cold and warm degree
and other forms of atmospheric lies
- my heart replied -
and I was surely answered.

Of course November came with fungal thoughts:
those tonsured minds uplifting from the soil
to teach us all those things we dare not learn.

But even then with sunlight in retreat
and silken snares to shimmer and deceive
with all their sheer geometries of light
my sentience could hear and touch and see
the taste that synaesthesia completes
with fog and frost.

I can smell the loss that surely has to come
down that once path that's now and never then:
the ferment and the fragrance of the earth -
that urgency of something in the past
that still inspires.

And ice - well what is that - but all these stars
that glitter in the grass where all is born.
This month of incarnation and the dark

that holds me still enthralled but not apart
from thoughts of gold and frankincense
and myrrh and Lenten flowers.

December when for three unholy days
the sun stands still
cannot deny Eostre all her dreams
and as the host of light slopes down the hill
into the red-recumbency of dusk

I hear the cuckoo call from some far wood
the Angelus that elevates the will
and my old bones.

ML

## ESSEX EARTHQUAKE 1884

Nine twenty a.m. on a bright Tuesday morning
Peldon and Abberton, Wivenhoe way,
Sunny the sky, as it came without warning,
The rumbling, the thunder below on that day…

Underground movements are rare to this nation,
Earthquakes are something just few of us see.
Shaken and stirred was an awed population –
'Storm-tossed like boats on an earth-coloured sea.'

In less than a minute some twelve hundred buildings
were damaged or shattered by waves in the round.
Churches lost battlements. Towers and spires,
Broken and rent, tumbled down to the ground.

Chimneys came smashing through roofs they'd surmounted,
Walls cracked and masonry clattered about.
People ran outdoors, confused and haunted.
Earth rose and fell as the shockwaves spread out.

Farmer and horses in fields shook and stumbled.
Little Wigb'rough's tower lost many a tier.
Fissures on Mersea. The Peldon mill tumbled.
At Southend a fisherman fell off the pier…

RH

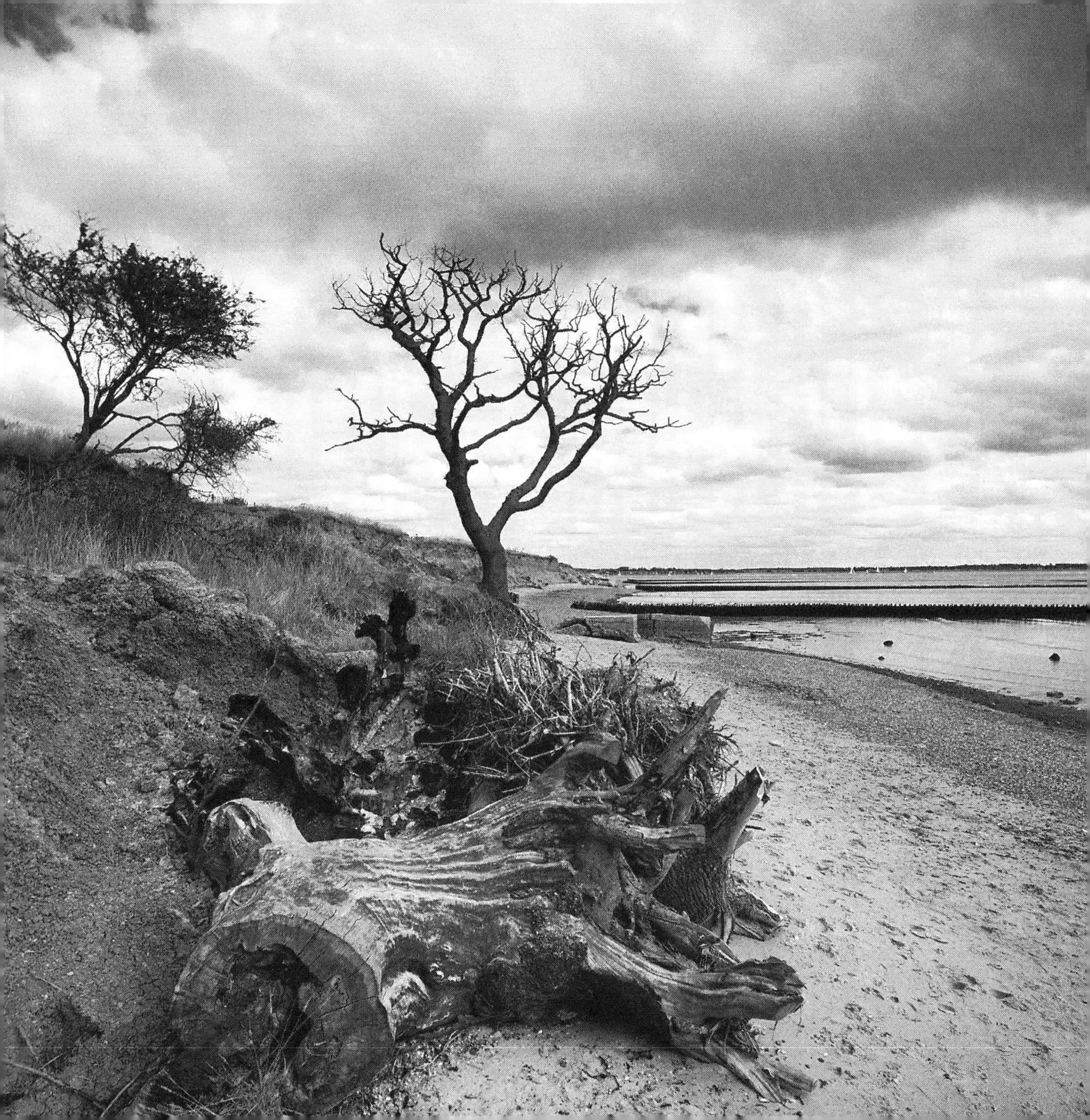

## MERSEA ISLAND

Perhaps not picturesque: but beautiful
in its own way. The grey mudflats
stretch to the grey horizons. Green slime

scuttles with green crabs and the smell is that
of pearls and oysters. Men with 'J Class' minds
study the rising tide and boats in gullies

rock within the cradle of the sea. Brent geese
bob like black buoys in the fairways
and herring gulls trumpet the sound of the west.

Mudflats, bladder-wrack, saltings: these are
the words that move me. The curlews'
                double lament
drifts over distant bars and my heart's cold
compass swings in the gimbals of the moon.

ML

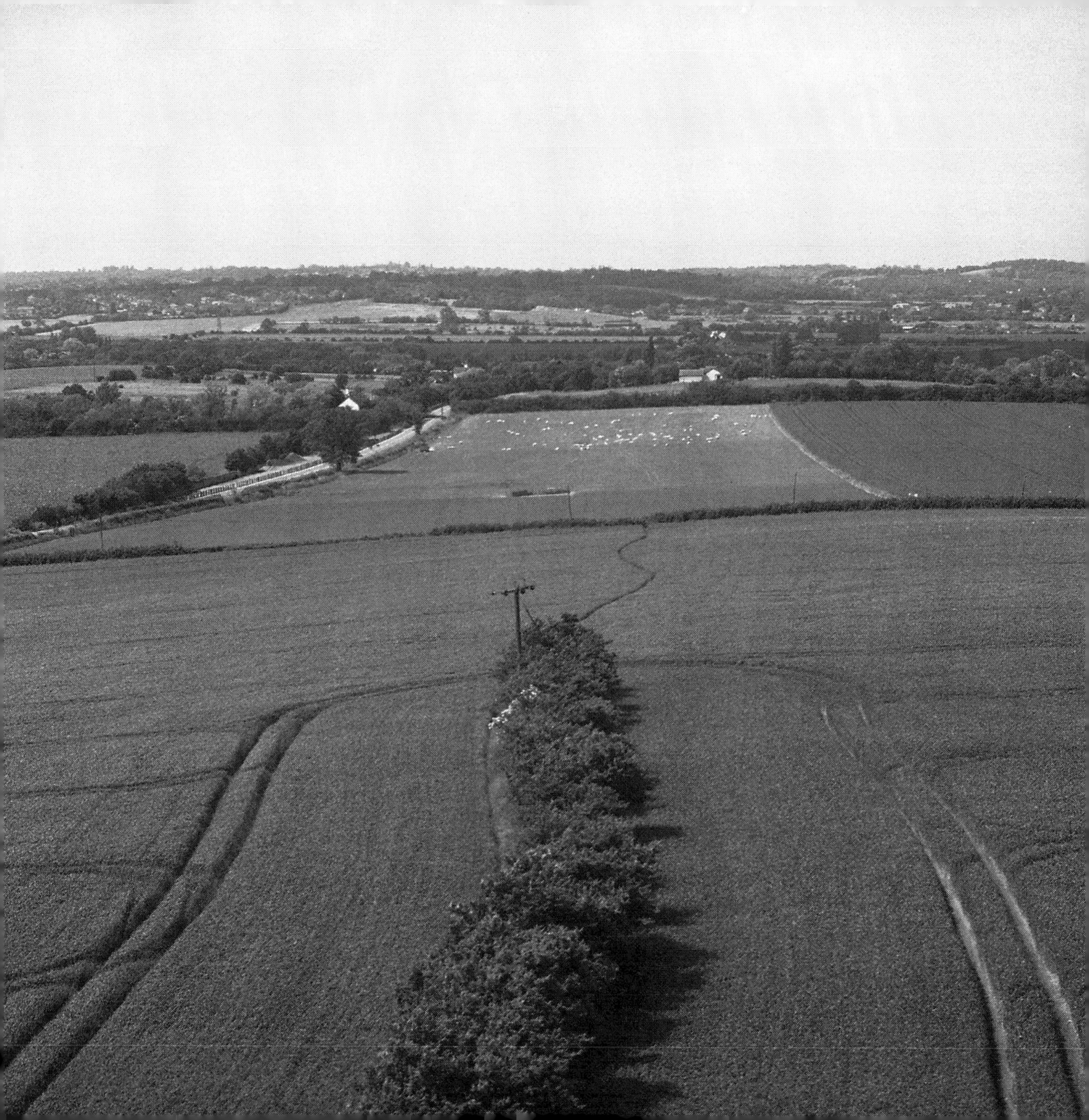

## ESSEX HISTORY

East Saxon land of ancient lore
From Stansted to the North Sea shore,
From Dedham to the mighty Thames
You'll find a land beset with gems:

From Bradwell, where the Saint with grace
Built, straddling Celt and Roman space,
To Benfleet, where the Wessex men
Cleared out marauding Vikings' den.

To Hedingham, where Norman Squires
Would warm their bums on English fires,
Ensconced themselves in walls of might
And ruled as by a conqueror's right.

To Felsted, where the schemer lies
Enriched in marble enterprise,
Unjustly resting on his deeds,
Resplendent flaunting lies and greeds.

To Rochford, where a king's desire
Ensnared the virgin to aspire,
To grace the fickle royal bed –
And lose her pretty little head…

RH

## FIELDS OF VISION

(The Battle of Assundune - 1016)

There is more down this lane than nature:
There is time and timelessness, blackberry
Preserves, elderberry wine, pictures

Of the past in fermentation. There are tracks
between the fields; ways between wheat
Winding towards the Crouch, a battlefield

Long-buried under pasture. Victory
Or defeat; what matters? There is verdure,
Larksong; salt-laden tides, springs and neaps.

The cognoscenti of the picturesque
Ramble this way and that: consult their guides,
Maps, field-books. There is more than nature

Down this lane: more than the cabbage-whites,
Their double helices, territory.
The distended sun - corpuscular - subsides

As barn-owls quarter starlight in the east
And love's unknowing moon: ascends -
decreases.

ML

**MUCKING**

With will to conquer came the Roman might
On Claudius' orders landed on that shore.
Superior forces pushing to the fore,
Well trained, well-armed and spoiling for a fight

On Kentish beach the legions came to land.
The foreign foe, they battled not by stealth
To conquer England and to steal its wealth.
Yet English fighters came to make their stand:

Caratacus faced battle-eager host
With spear and chariot to defend their pride,
The men of England tried to stem the tide –
They were no equals and their cause was lost.

Forlorn withdrawal was the only way
Across the Thames at Mucking led their road
Familiar sandbanks stood for bridge or boat
By shield of night, to fight another day,

Unbowed, unbroken, while the legions bayed
They waded through the Thames, the tide was low.
Their chariots fleet, they carried spear and bow,
Retreating army, with their wounded weighed…

RH

**MUCKING & MESSING**

If you love Essex, you'll love Mucking:
if you love Mucking you'll love messing -
Messing and Mucking are a blessing
        for lovers of Essex.

Mucking had muck but now it doesn't -
it has skylarks and seals, porpoises and fritillaries, avocets and harriers

and Messing, I suppose,
but I'll keep you guessing for a while,
has crops and cottages, copses and cuckoos, bluebells and anemones

        - but now I've told you -
            what a mess!

Enough of the muck and the mess
today at Mucking by the Thames I'm thinking of Messing
and when the sun rests its hot and sparkling countenance of the waters
                like rippling gold

I'm in mind of the cornfields at Messing
            - or is it wheat?

What's in a name or a jest when mucking about or messing with words
anything can happen, not just muck or mess
even more, even less, even poetry
            - perhaps -
            who knows?

ML

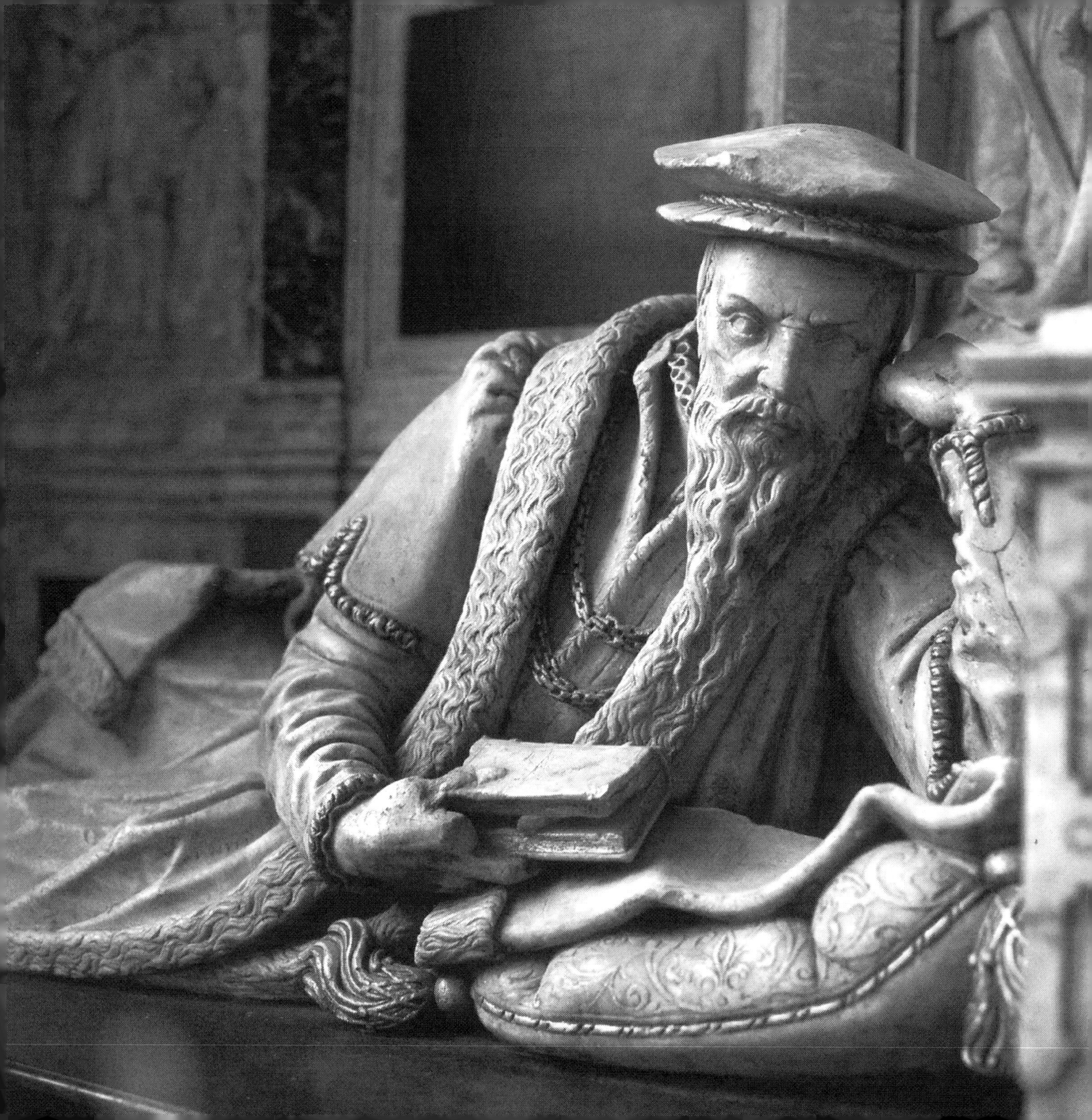

## THE SILENCE OF PLESHEY CASTLE

Shakespeare remembered that sad sad place
That lies amidst its village, rarely trod.
Of its hustle and bustle there's barely a trace,
As if cursed and shunned and by history forgot'.

The bailey lies empty, the bald motte stands bare.
The ancient brick bridge spans the moat quite forlorn.
You'll find no stockade, no proud tower there –
From the home of the Gloucesters' the heart has been torn.

But once here were hunts and fine ladies and knights,
A chapel, bright gardens and bowers' of scent,
Milady Eleanor enjoyed the delights
With her husband Thomas of royal descend.

Her husband the Duke and his brother at pains
Had ruled the land when the King was a child,
Brought honour to England in foreign campaigns,
But old habits – and intrigue – die hard and stay wild…

For the king was of age now and proving his worth
And his uncle a thorn in his eyes –
In 1397 he tracked him to earth
To Pleshey, while planning his uncle's demise.

Persuaded old Gloucester to follow his train
Back to London, to honour and glory –
Transported instead to Calais and slain
Out of sight, in a deed foul and hoary.

RH

**A STAG AMONGST THE PHEASANTS**
(Mark's Hall - Coggeshall)

A stag strides out across the land:
close to the hedgerow -
close to the feeding pheasants.

Its antlers catch the velvet of the sky
and sunset gilds its tines
with mythic gold.

The pheasants lift their bright enamelled heads:
legends in their own exotic right -
priests of the Advent season.

Mistletoe and magic stir my mind
as this cold dusk elaborates on stars
and flighting ducks draw down the crescent moon

on silvered wings.
A Christmas card, a print, a dream in oils:
something that can touch without a hand

and move the heart to moments out of time
in this cruel landscape.
I can almost hear the frost:

the powdered glass that crisps the evening sward
when footsteps are the poacher and the fox
and light is slaughtered.

ML

**BENFLEET (BEAMFLEOT)**
**BATTLE HYMN AD 893**

Speak, ye chronicles of old,
Benfleet's story must be told.
From the shores of far-off time
Pluck the harp and sing this rhyme:

Sea-men blond and keen for plunder
Came to tear this land asunder.
Dragonships with force and stealth
Carried off the country's wealth.

Hardship followed where they passed.
England's hero came at last
From the bogs of Athelney –
Raised his standard strong and free.

To this young and shattered nation
Alfred was the inspiration.
Call on Thegn and Earl and Sax',
Blunt the pirates' bloody axe.

Men of will and warriors hoary
Took up arms for England's glory.
To pursue and halt and rout
Alfred sought the Vikings out.

Water sweet and harbour fair,
Benfleet was the sea-men's lair.
Haesten 'Niger' led the host,
Hero of the mead-halls' toast.

Over ditch and rampart thrust,
For revenge and glory lust.
Draw the anvil's heat-forged blades
And return the raiders' raids.

Danish shield meets Saxon spear
Send the fiends to flight in fear.
Soak the Downs with heathen blood.
Burn their ships on Benfleet's mud.

Haesten, plundering abroad
Still escaped the Saxon sword.
Wife and hostages were taken
While he left his fort forsaken.

When the battle-din fell quiet
Odin wild and Thor retired.
Benfleet and its harbour-creek
Were blessed by Mary, virgin meek.

On that bloody, ancient spot
Rose a sacred house of God –
Claimed for all eternity
By peace and Christianity.

RH

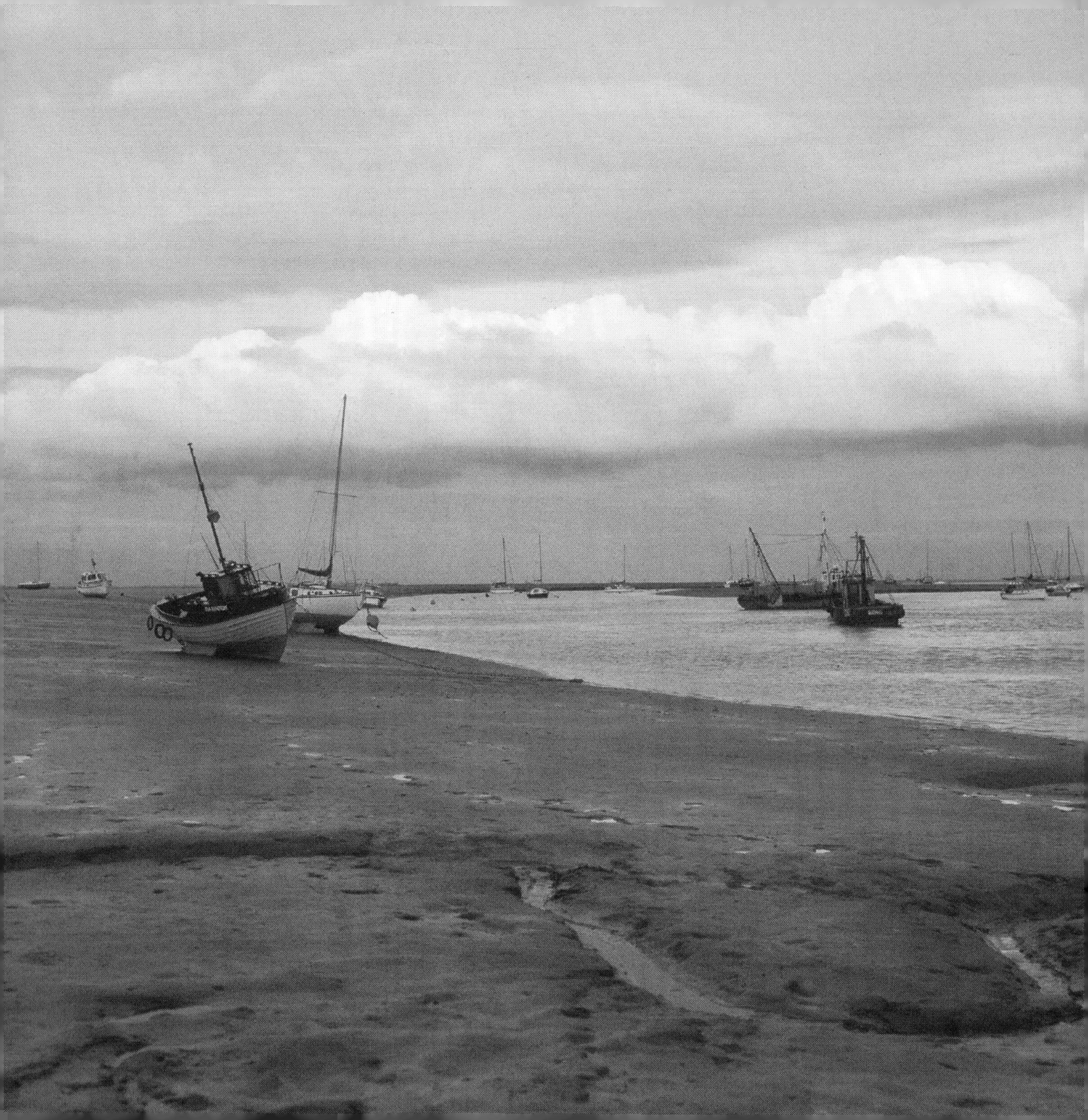

## HADLEIGH RAY

The slipway is half submerged: slopes into
The cold, grey creek - as if to make submission
To the moon whose gravity and day-assuming
Skull - is framed in blue. There is a misted

Ambience that chills as curlews call
Their solitary notes and ghosted
Music shivers with the tide. The old seawall
Curves towards the castle from the coast

Where ancient heights are grazed or sown with wheat
And thoughts of spring return again to winter.
There are a few new shoots - a few new leaves:
But mostly there are geese on spectral wings

Who fail to set their bearing for the north
And summer's tundra. A shelduck laughs:
An eerie sound from some unearthly source
That takes the mind through fathoms to the past

On this bleak shore. A Viking longship draws
Its shallow draught towards a Saxon inlet
In the marsh where timbers rot and nets are stored
Away - and all is silence. I am perplexed:

Where are the warriors - the fishermen -
The farmers? Is this time or timelessness?
A curlew sounds its isolate amen
As April's early tide begins to rise

Across the flats. What century is this?
The crows - that could be ravens - taunt the gulls
As wooden craft - reflected - lift and list
And ghastly lights: illuminate - their hulls.

ML

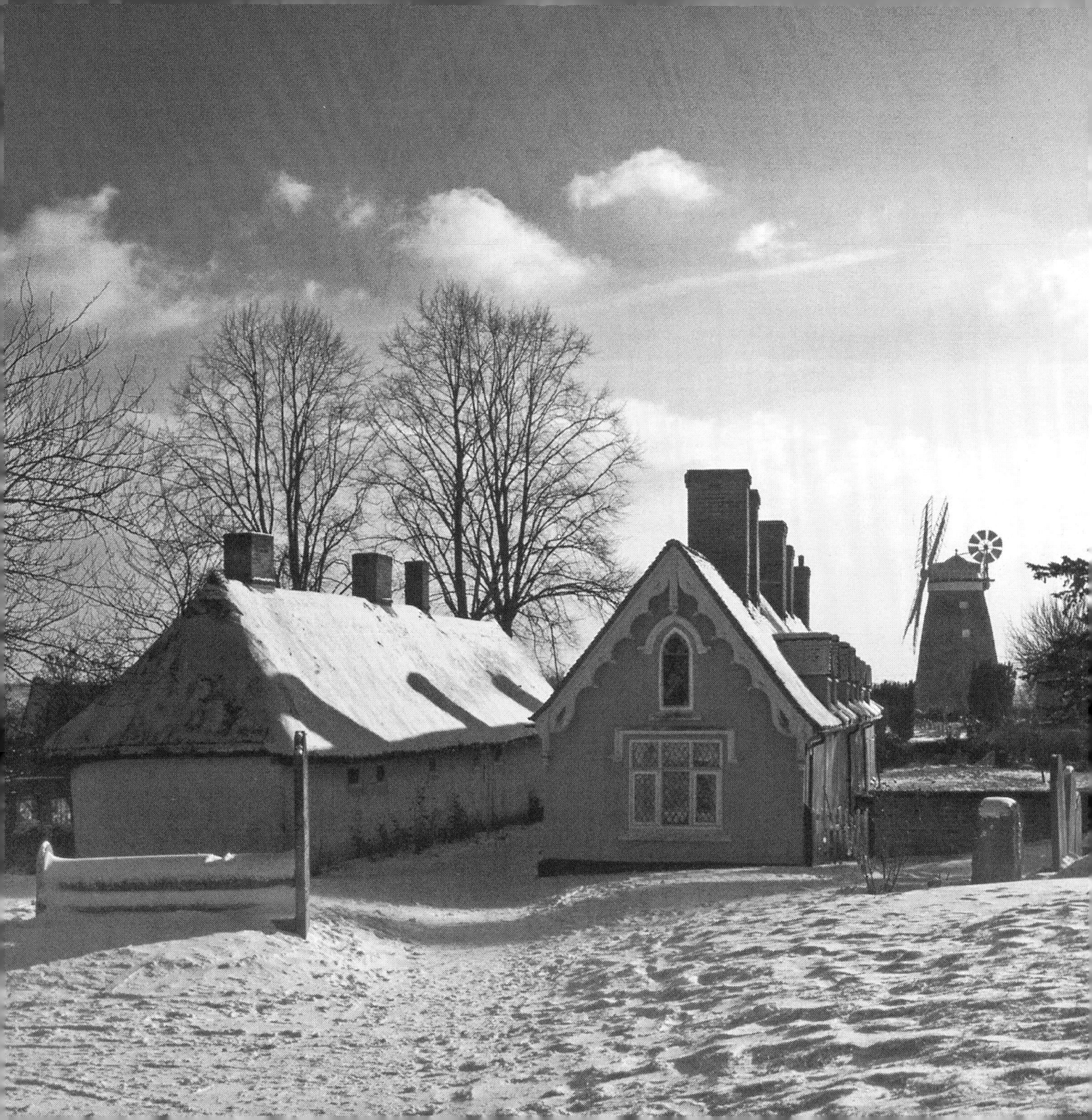

## THAXTED

In twelve-eighty-seven one Richard de Taxte
Was known as a hafter in the village of Thaxted.
In thirteen-ninety the Guildhall was built
By the Guild of Cutlers who made knife, axe and hilt

And halberds and surgeons' tools of renown,
When Stoney Road still was the main road in town.
Upon the old cobbles tradition fared well
And harmony, music and dance cast their spell.

The Morris Ring formed here in nineteen eleven,
Since then the town 's been the Morris Men's heaven.
The organ was played by a Maestro magician,
Whose music took wings over craft and tradition.

He soared to *'The Planets',* we listen entranced…
A blue plaque marks mortar this genius enhanced.
'Gustav Holst, Composer', a master of sound.
His house and its garden were fertile ground.

A *'Choral Symphony'* grew among flowers,
A *'Festival Chorus'* – his music is ours:-
*'Our Church-bells in Thaxted at Whitsuntide say,*
*Come all you good people and put care away…'*

RH

## PEEWITS AND PLANETS

As it darkens
the lights beyond the saltings
scintillate – like stars.

The sky, though cloudless,
is pink and blue and green –
portentous it seems of frost
and even fog.

A skein of brent geese
unravels
and settles on the mudflats.

You can hear them 'barking'
as curlew 'bubble'
and lapwing pitch
their piercing, high, nomenclature.

No stars, no moon, as yet –
we await the reflective ones
that circle the ecliptic and the spheres.

Mars, Mercury, Jupiter,
you can hear them if you listen.

They sound like gulls
that glitter in the frost

or widgeon in the fogbanks
out to sea –
webbed and whistling.

ML

**ZEPPELIN L33**

They had dropped their bombs on London from their floating Zeppelin.
Bi-planes, circling, found their target, broke the leviathan's skin.

Captain Böcker and his comrades, on returning to their home,
Losing weight, turned back to Essex, lest they perish in the foam.

Circling Peldon, Little Wigborough was the place of their demise.
Landing safely in a meadow, came the terror from the skies.

One last order, one last duty – their gas-filled craft must be destroyed!
Lit up field and sky for miles on that warm September night.

As the crew came to enquire for the road to Colchester,
In her cottage Mrs. Lewis cowered frightened by the stair.

A policeman in his civvies, like Dad's Army, came to see
And accepted their surrender, thirteen crew and officers three.

Postmistress at Little Wigborough quite refused to keep them there.
No-way outside business hours. No-one told her to prepare…

So they marched the Strood to Mersea, where the Military stepped in,
Took them to the island's church hall to reflect on fate and sin.

It is said, that Sunday morning, locals came to play and sing
With accordion and fervour: 'Rule Britannia' and 'God Save the King'.

RH

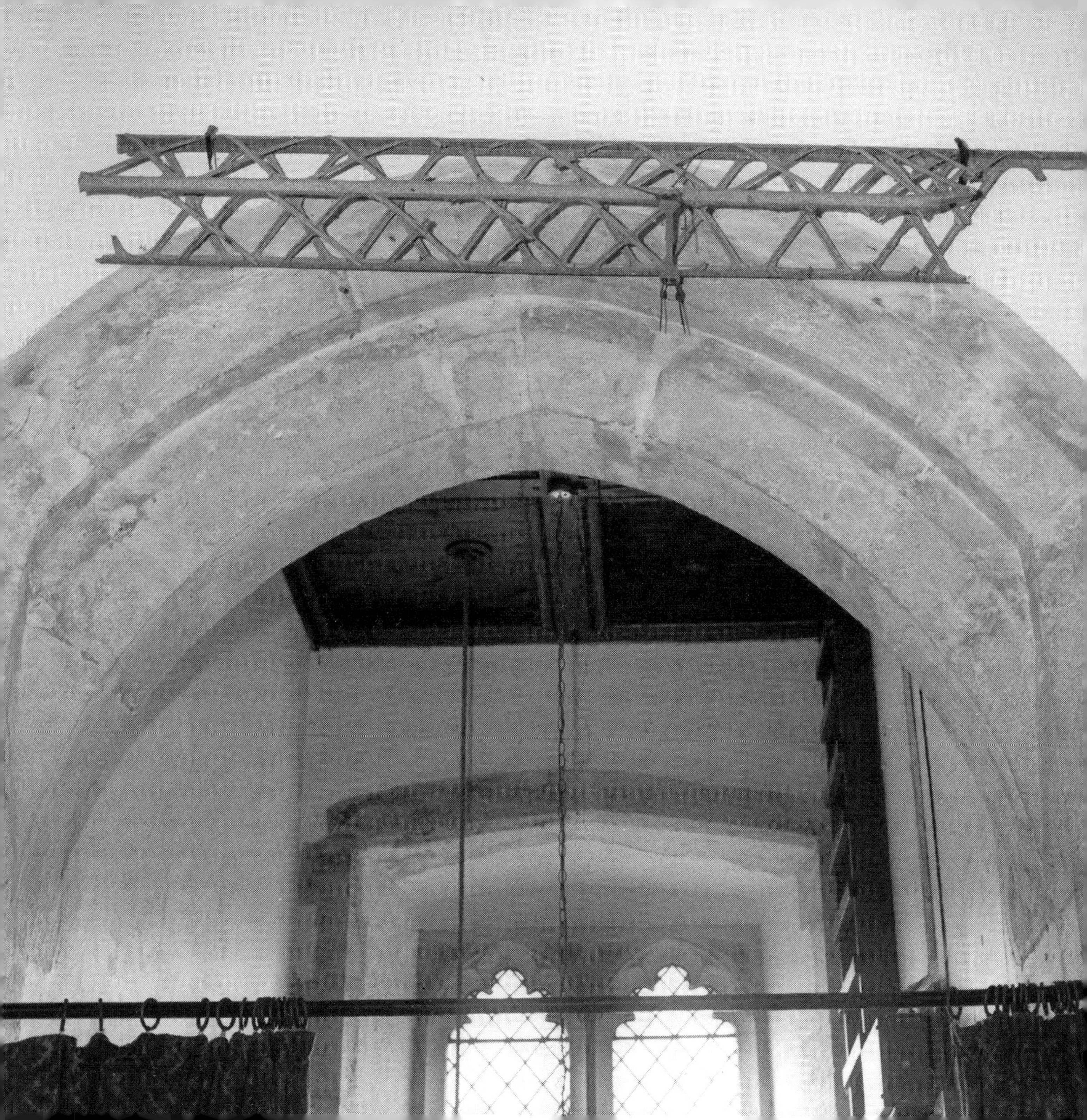

**PROPHECY AT ST STEVEN'S**
(Little Wigborough)

This is the end of summer - end of time:
As down the air the leaves begin to fall
And all we saw as roses steeped in light
Inclines to darkness. How these trees appal:

Despite the gold, the flare and spark of yellow,
We cannot see the beauty - as the fire -
Consumes our hearts. Even the swallow
Leaves us: leaves us to the maple's dying

Scarlet: the fungal skulls of mushrooms
In the fields - the sun's interment. Rooks
and daws
Are making for their roost as dusk subsumes
The moment and the mind with all the laws

Of winter - and their cries. The end - of time:
The lichen on the churchyard's crumbling wall
Is tarnished by the prophecy of night
And every leaf: that flickers - as it falls.

ML

**SUMMER CLOUDS**

Knights on white chargers, their pennants
unfurled,
Riding in majesty over my world,

Changing and floating in oceans of blue –
Imagination makes anything true.

Three-masted schooners that shape-shift
and tease,
White fluffy sails just blow in the breeze.

Heads of old sailors and gargoyles galore,
Pale and carbuncled, so far from a shore

Change into lions and white woolly sheep,
Merging and growing to mountaintops steep.

Ghost ships and monsters and pale-
blossomed trees,
Snow-owls, white eagles and doves sail my seas,

Giants and trolls from my stories pass by,
High in the blue of my summertime sky…

RH

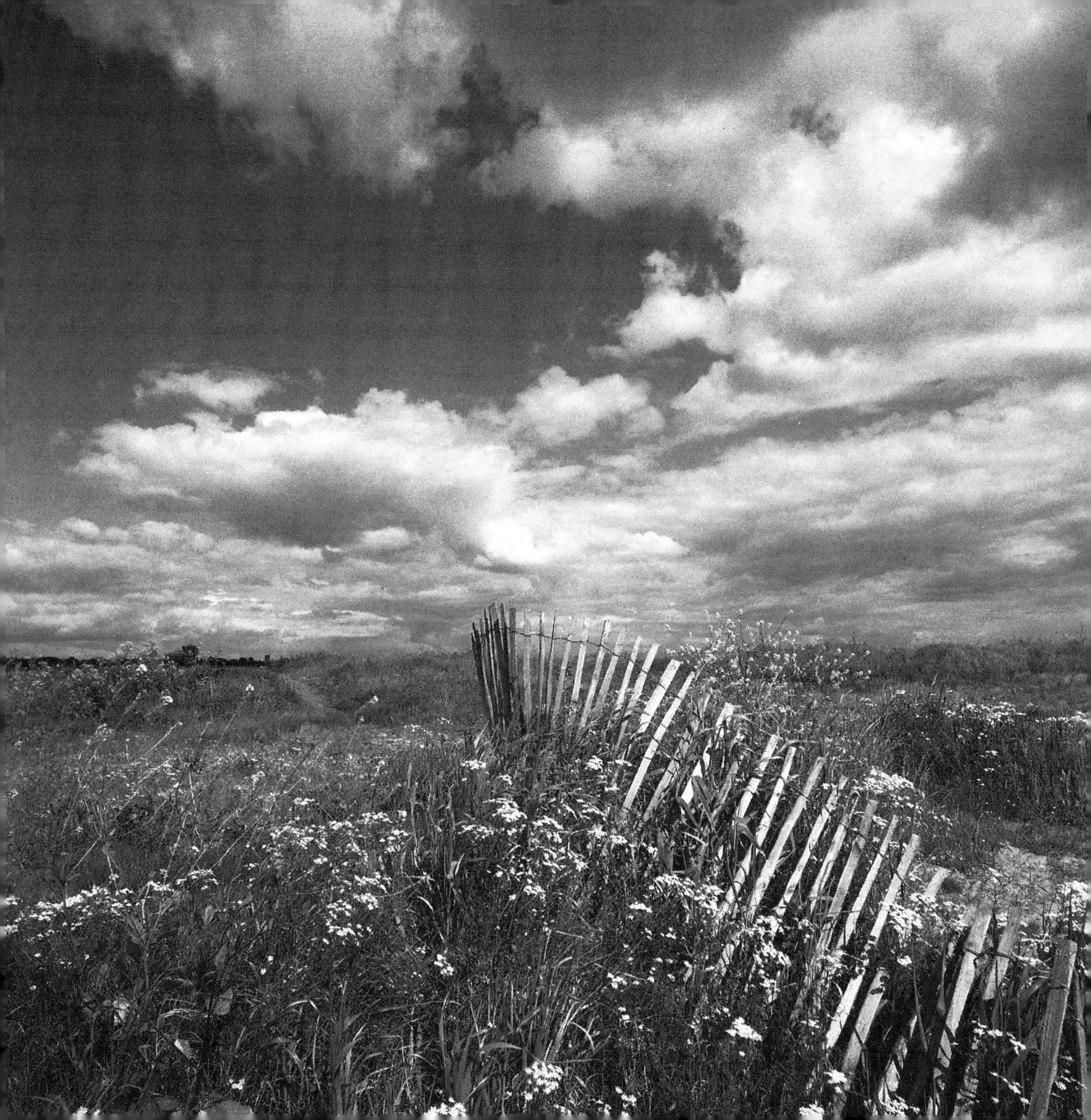

## CUCKOO LAND

We do not own it, but it's ours:
The subtle changes are our property -

The endless transformations of the clouds
Filling the coffers of a stateless summer.

The birds have territory to defend -
    Parameters of song.

We turn our pockets out:
Ignore the fences -
Belong to no-one but ourselves.

We feed on love, like bees
  That drown in pollen.

Yet still I doubt the coinage of the flowers:
My spendthrift words -
The tongue's unsound collateral.

ML

## THE TIDAL RIVER

Do not wander alone
                    where the cliff has no stone,
Do not wander the strand at the Ness.
I'm reluctant to say,
                    you may cry, you may pray,
But I'd rather not stay, I confess.
Do not wander alone
                    where the cliff meets the foam,
Do not wander alone on that strand.
If you love a good fright,
                    at the turn of the tide
You are prone to the demons' demand.
Do not wander alone
                    where the green groynes groan
On the mud that will stop your retreat.
There are fiends that will suck,
                    pull you down in the muck –
You'll look funny without toes or feet.

There is no escaping at speed.
From the demons that think you're a treat.

RH

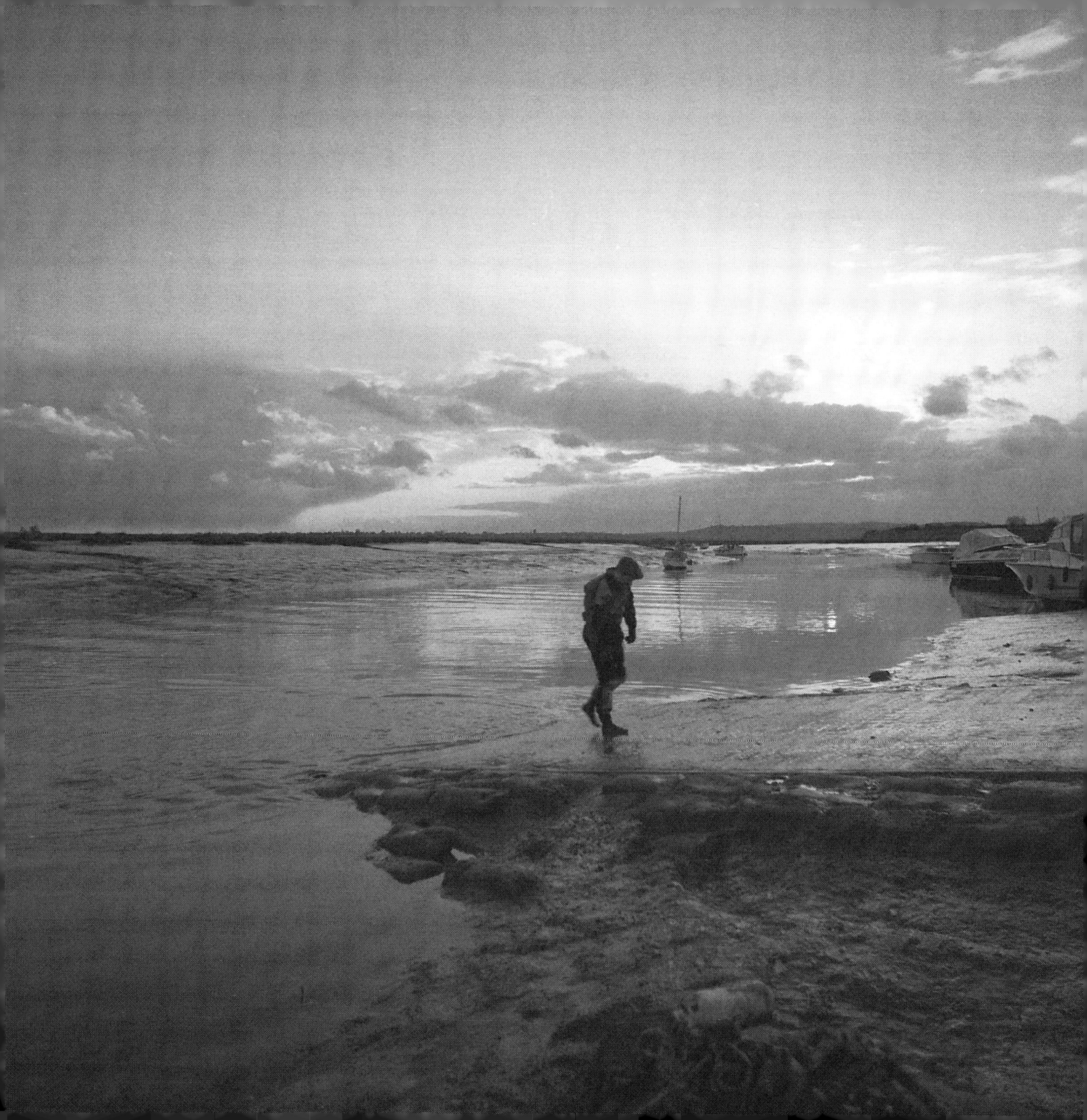

## BAIT DIGGER – TWO TREE ISLAND CHRISTMAS MORNING

Three ships – not exactly:
Leigh Ray and Tewkes Creek
wind their grey and convoluted track
between the Christmas banks of mud and sand
where bladder wrack and eelgrass frame the day
  in wreaths of darkness.

One isolated figure, dressed in black,
squelches through the ooze and seems to say
that loneliness is human and the lack of winter light.

A curlew flutes, and sound, its sad refrain,
floats across the sandbanks and the flats
to where the sun, a star in all but name,
illuminates a trinity of gulls
between the clouds.

ML

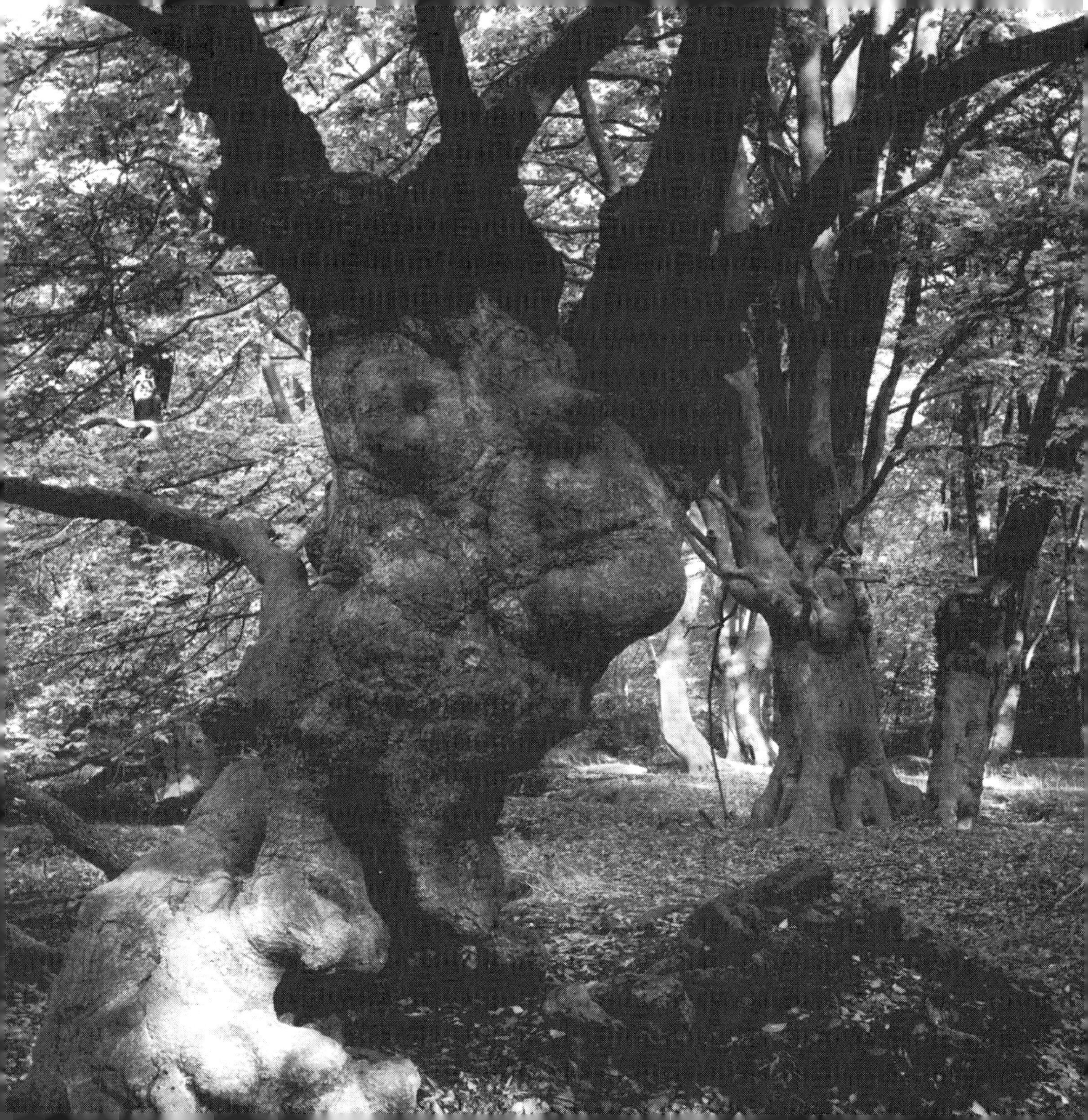

## WILDWOODS' RAVE

When they held a rave in Turpin's Cave
The Elfins danced with Joy
And Fred and Sal and Sid, their pal
And all that hoi-polloy.

They danced in line and they danced in pairs
And a ring-o'-roses that led to tears
When Morgan the Organ and Hip the Harp
Played a hop and a jig in A Major sharp,
While the Leprechauns and Will-o'-the-wisps
Drank foxglove juice and crunched their crisps
'Til the early dawn, when they saw the light.

And a Faerie Sprite kissed a Troll 'Good Night'
And Rumpelstiltskin and Dwarfs galore –
(I am bad at maths, there might well be more).
Until everyone fell asleep where they stood –

And they put down roots in that magic wood
In the strangest shapes. On the woodland floor
You can find them still, but they dance no more.
And if you walk in that whispering place,
You'll see many a frown on the sleeping face
Of a tree or a shrub in a twisted stance
Where the Wildwood crowd held
        their very last dance.

RH

## DRYADS

When I'm in the woods
I feel different:

The breezes speak to me -
Whispers - perhaps -

But nonetheless a language.
I still believe in dryads:

Childhood pictures
Of trees with faces

Seem more than mythical -
Spirits - entities.

It's not in the mind:
Known by the grain

Of the heart -
Xylem and phloem

Of an inner feeling.
Squirrels are their messengers:

Sprites In the leaf-light
Of a dim reflection -

Grey and condensing
Like the breath on glass.

ML

**HOW DOES IT FEEL**

When butterflies first
Rise from the dew
Sparkling and new
        How does it feel

When lambs on the fells
New-born in May
Gambol and play
        How does it feel

When summer inspires
Skylarks at noon
Warble their tune
        How does it feel

When birds fly through rain
Tumble and reel
Plummet and wheel
        How does it feel?

HOW DOES IT FEEL

When dolphins cry out
Struggle and weep
Poisoned the deep
        How does it feel

When seagulls are trapped
Covered in oil
Humans despoil
        How does it feel

When elephants die
Ivory greed
Pays for the deed
        How does it feel

Out hunting the stag
Badger and hare
Caught in the snare
        How does it feel?

HOW DOES IT FEEL

When baby first lies
Soft at your breast
Smiling at rest
        How does it feel

When 'baby' grows tall
Steals his first kiss
Worry and bliss
        How does it feel

When spirit breaks free
Travel so far
Follow your star
        How does it feel

When 'baby' leaves home
Futures to find
Leaves you behind
        How does it feel?

RH

## MAY DAY

Too slight to drown; too weak to fly away,
A moth or some-such thing without renown
Just struggles with the water's surface tension.

It's May, and the river's perfect calm
Repeats the day through each inverted image.

A field of rape is swallowed by a wood
And the sky is crazed by cirrus under blue.

A cuckoo - in its repetitious way -
Intrudes across the distance and the haze;

Too slight to drown, too weak to fly away,
A moth or some-such thing without renown
Diffuses into circles; into waves.

ML

## THE VIXEN'S GARDEN

The vixen came haltingly down the lawn,
Sniffing the air in the new light of dawn.
She stood tall and proud, a boon to fox-kind,

Asserting her birth right with future in mind.
Her long thin nose was testing the air
To be certain of safety – there's no danger here.

A little one followed her, leaping with joy
To grab her attention and make her its toy,
Rumbled and stumbled and gambolled and chased

Under the shrubs, round the fruit trees it raced.
The vixen responded and nuzzled the cub
And they jumped and cavorted and stopped for a rub.

She seems quite at home, she begs no-one's pardon,
Certainly not ours, the guests in her garden…

RH

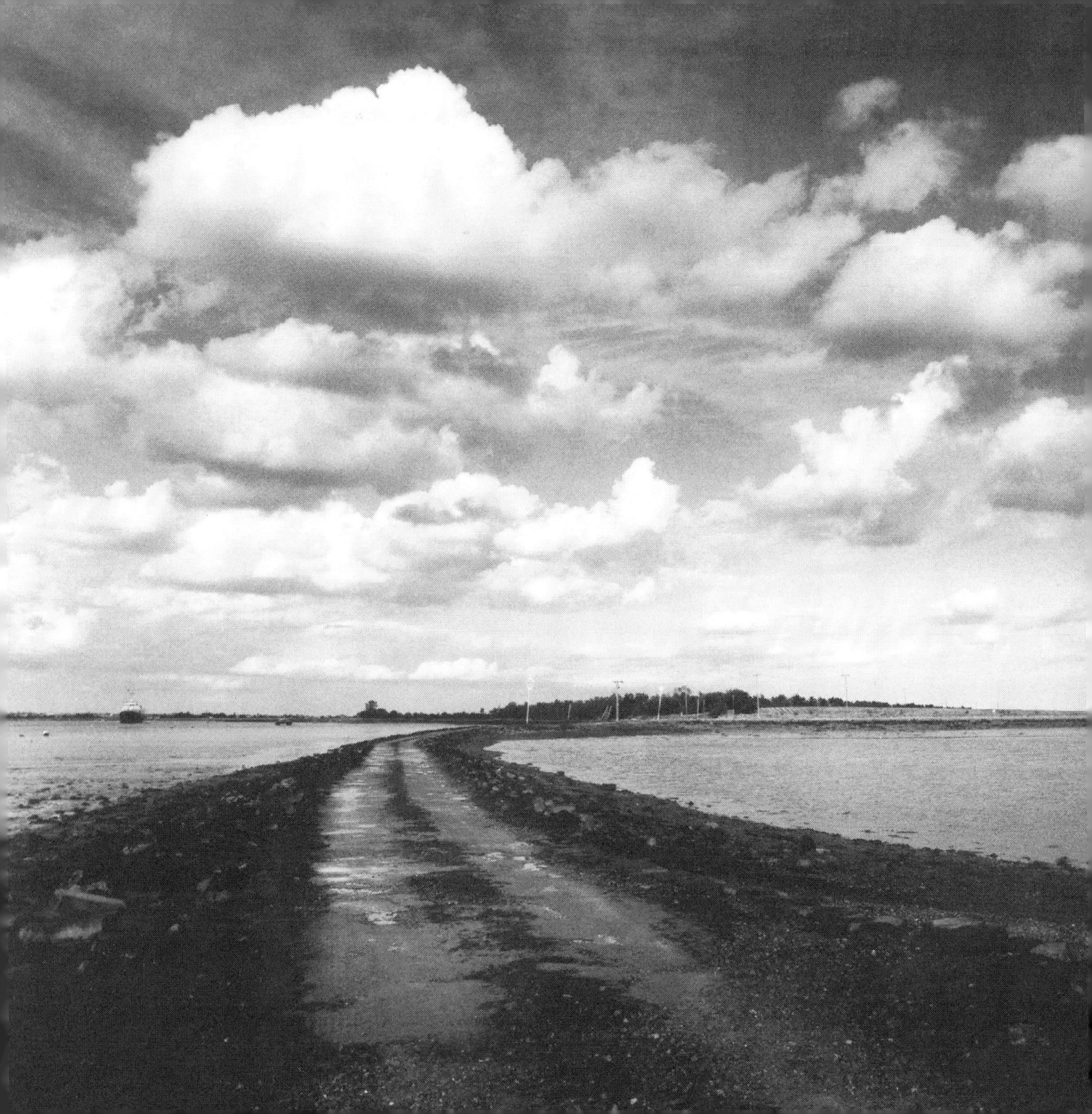

## DECEMBER HUNT

After the hounds
and the horses
the water is cloudy.

The scent is lost
and the day drowns
in its own darkness.

A scarlet cloak
stands out
across the fields

and the fox lies safely
in some distant cover.

Rooks and the first stars
reveal themselves
as opposites at dusk

and the moon
like a silver stirrup
curves through the heavens
with the earth in harness.

ML

## A TOAST TO ESSEX

To mud-born marshes, rivers wide,
Subordinate to time and tide.

With creek and dam and sandbank vast
And haunting ghosts of battles past,

Where geese and gulls in silver flight
Surround the coast at eventide.

And while those gentle winds prevail,
With creaking plank and russet sail

The barges home to Maldon's quay
From river dark and angry sea.

The saffron blanket, heavy soil.
The sailor's call. The farmer's toil.

The Viking's sword, the Saxon's plough.
To Essex! Fame and fortune grow!

RH

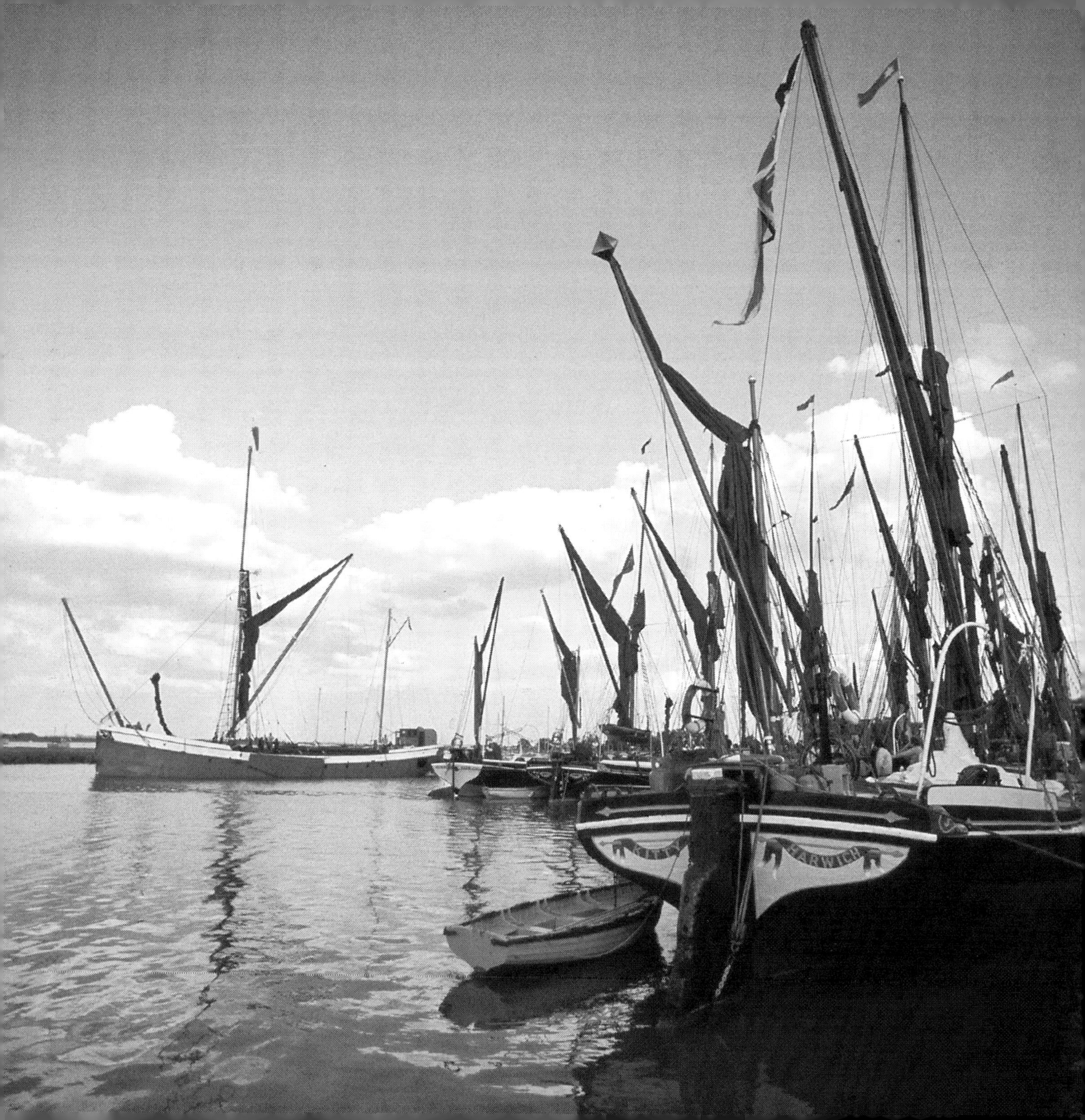

**COOK'S YARD - MALDON**

Still at work:
shaping the sprits, bending planks -
plying the trade of a tide at ebb.

The barges wait in restoration's hand -
like days returned to worry with their flotsam.

Buildings to landward
climb and cluster in contorted ranks.

A church stands beacon on a rising slope
and the shelving shore
curves through the mooring into banks of grey.

A gull breaks silence from a listing mast
then dives to the delving of its own reflection.

Air in a soft furl
fathoms the angles of a standing rig

and the sea-sung music
swells through the saltings on a wave that passes.

ML

## THE CUNNING MAN

When the Wizard walked these acres
Ever watchful. Herb and heal.
All the creatures of his maker
Knew the worth of his appeal:-

*'Mr. Murrell, can you help me?*
*Can you help me, Mr. Murls?*
*I have lost my father's fobwatch.*
*Do you know who stole my pearls?'*

*'Mr. Murrell, I am anxious.*
*That's why I appeal to you.*
*My intended still avoids me,*
*Can you tell him what to do?'*

*'Will you send another potion*
*That will make my stummic heal?*
*I have taken what you sent me –*
*Now I've got a funny feel…'*

*'My poor horse has got the colic,*
*Can you make him pull his load?*
*And my cow has dried up udders.*
*Should I boil a frog and toad?'*

*'Does my husband have a lover?*
*Oh, I think he's gone astray.*
*Will he leave me? Can you make him*
*See the error of his way?'*

*'She is evil. My suspicion*
*Is, she doesn't wish me well…*
*Can you make your special bottle*
*To explode my neighbour's spell?'*

RH

## THE ESOTERIC ANGLER

He knew the river well -
Was fluent with its meanings.

Though asked to tell
His answers were evasive -
Kept to the margins,
Like a shoal of secrets.

Equivocation was his lure -
Meanderings his disposition.

No one for sure could
Penetrate the depths -
Fathom the contents
In his mesh of words.

Once hooked and held secure,
He waited till you leapt
Towards the light;

Then slowly with
A deftness that procures,
He drew you in
And ministered the priest.

*Priest: blunt instrument for dispatching fish*

ML

## BEAUTIFUL OCTOBER MORNING,

Clean and crisp and touched by mist.
Pale blue Canvey in the distance
Melting slowly, sunlight-kissed.

Would that life could follow daydreams.
Golden glow obscures truth.
Could this view but stay 'til evening.
Could this child retain its youth…

Speckled starlings, sparrows scratching,
Chasing, preening undeterred.
Magpie on its perch surveying –
Silence. Not a human word.

Beautiful October morning,
Clean and crisp and touched by mist.
Pale blue Canvey in the distance
Melting slowly, sunlight-kissed.

RH

## SAD SONGS & FALLEN ANGELS

Not the curlew's fluted double note:
the usual long and lingering lament across the flats -
but a bubbling, like the cuckoo in the spring,
when bluebells are a seascape of their own
    and stitchwort sparkles.

Now as grey October takes a hold
and tidal waters, monotone and slack,
bear the weight of geese
    in wide black rafts

  all thoughts of gold
are tarnished like the leaves
of hawthorn by the saltings and the wrack
    of seaborne flotsam.

Again the bubbling sound that ebbs and flows
along the winding gullies and the creeks
evolves and evanesces like the land
that forms and fails as sea frets
find the need to limit vision.

Alone along the curve of this seawall
I walk between obscurity's grey doors
and where the saltings meet the solemn ooze
the littorals, the shingle, and the shore,

the rush of geese uplifting on the wings
of gutturals and winter's cold reprise
are somehow like perdition's feathered score -
    fathomless and fallen.

ML

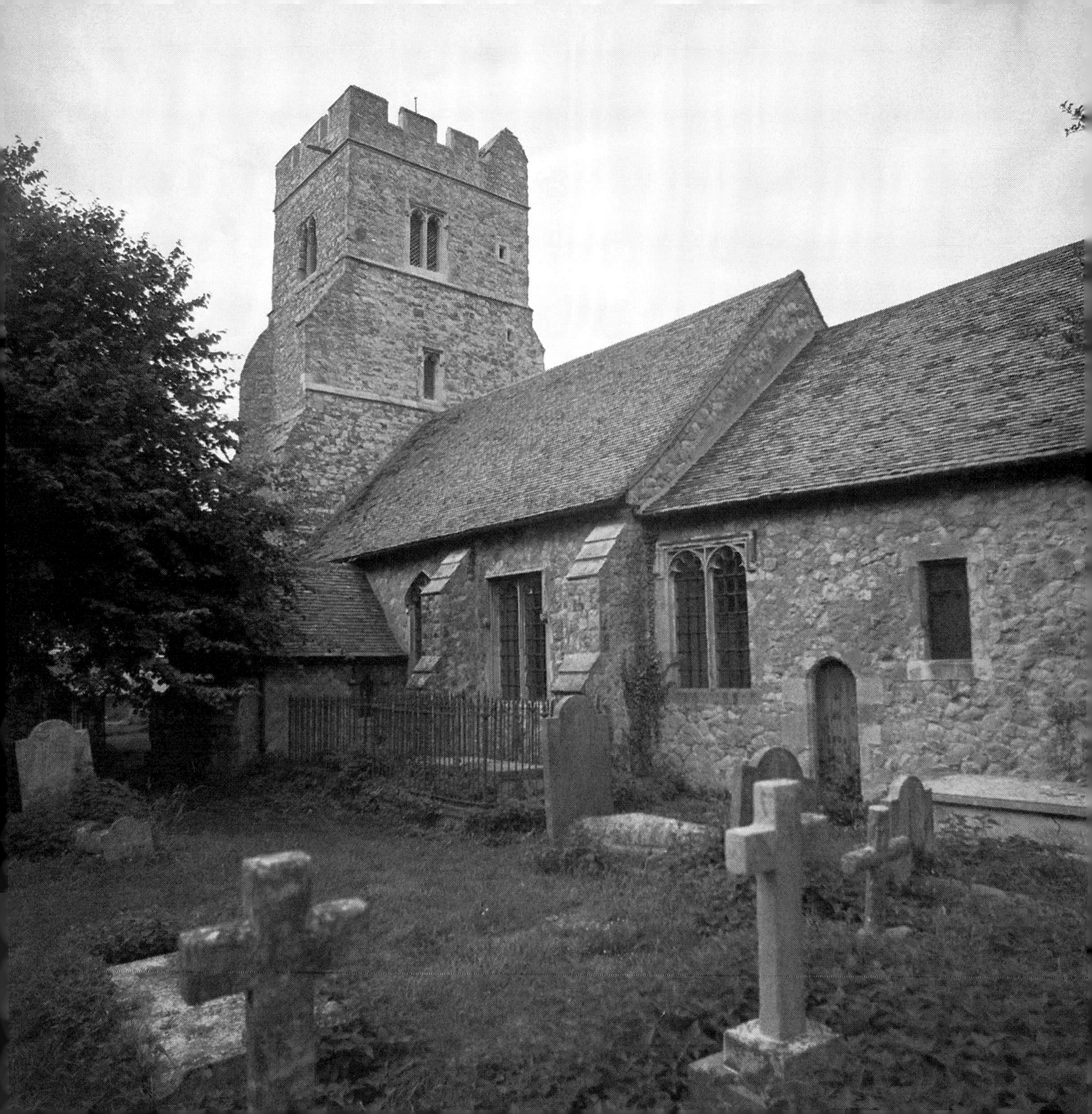

**BLISS**

This is my bit of heaven,
This precious spot on earth.
A softly chair, a splendid view,
A coffee mug to see me through
And pen and paper free at hand –
My Venice and my Samarkand.

The mind can dream and take to flight
And soar, explore each sound and sight.
The mind can travel all those places
Remembered or imagined, traces

The journey of my unclipped wings,
Where fancy takes to joyous springs
In burning deserts, mountains steep.
No pain, no worries where I leap
With youthful grace from star to stars,
Collecting bliss in apple jars.

Alone, or else with splendid friends
We savour life and buck the trends,
Share lively views and parry words
Like fire-forged and tempered swords…

Or rest among the chamomile
Close by some rustic country stile.
A butterfly's unfettered joy,
A kingfisher's dramatic ploy –
I am its speed, the north-wind's force
I am the ocean, plot its course –

And then, in this imagined bliss
You enter softly with a kiss.

RH

**A SKYLARK FOR ST ANDREW**

There is nothing left, not a leaf or a flower -
even the birds have fled this barren land.

There is brown and furrowed earth -
the anatomy of twigs and branches.

Other than that, just the grey prevailing
progress of the clouds across my mind

and then

- almost matter of fact -

without a thought
for the dull
and darkening
torment of the air

a skylark like a lyrical event
lifted a song beyond despair's great height

- like a star vibrating.

ML

## CRANEFLIES

It's autumn, my love, I tell you why: –
The craneflies are coming indoors to die.
Brief was their summer and briefer was spring.
It's only yesterday started their fling.

Through fear and fire his childhood bloomed,
For life and commerce the scholar groomed,
For the way ahead, for a future great,
All the things he yearned for, the plans he made…

As he tried his best, as the years passed by
The young man thought he would never die.
One day he wasn't so young anymore,
But he still kept trying, still pushing that door

At all the things that he meant to do.
Will there still be time? Will there still be you?
All the things we yearned for, the plans we made,
The dream we shared… Will it be too late?

It's autumn, my love, I tell you why: –
The craneflies are coming indoors to die.

RH

## GREAT DIVING BEETLE

"I've found a beetle," she said,
"I've put it in a jar for you to look at,
  It may be a Colorado."
Colorado it wasn't; not a pond in view
But it paddled in glass like a deep sea turtle.
A gem in a jar - a malachite broach
Edged and transected with translucent topaz.
Its bite can be painful it's said:
A heavy-jawed and voracious insect -
So I lifted it gently by the broad elytra.
The illusion of stone startled from
Its undersides - like a mottled onyx
Cleaved and polished into beige and brown.
The flattened legs rowed against a thin
  resistance
As they searched for the ocean of their
  own environs.
Where should I place it:
This animate jewel lost to the lustre of its
  bright aquatics -
How in the dryness of a drowning light
Can the lone exotic swim to the sanctum of its
  Own existence?

ML

## NATURE'S RHYTHM

Slow beats the primal heart of ebb and tide,
Of rise and fall, encroachment and retreat –
The narrow runnels grow to rivers wide,
To shrink again at ebb, a ceaseless beat.

And yet, for all its changes, there is constancy.
A rhythm, fixed, as day must follow night,
As sun will follow moon in silent potency
Returns the world, unerring, to the light.

The seasons have their place, the warmth returns.
The boy grows into man, from seed the tree.
The storms will pass and glorious sunshine burns
As time goes by in nature's constancy.

RH

## SNOW PIECE

At Barling Magna, across the fields of snow,
        with the evening sun
                red in the fire of returning frost

I saw the rooks fly low across the ground,
  Like living art distilled from pen and ink
      to counteract the whiteness of the page

And there without the hook of any sound
     I heard the written phoneme of a star
           expound the brittle languages of ice.

ML

## FOG-BOUND COMMUTER

(at South Benfleet railway station)

Here I stand, an island, breathing
In the midst of others, wheezing,
Platform-bound, depression-rife,
Shackled to a shunting life.

Leave the hearth, your friends, the local.
Listen to the tannoy's vocal.
Will the coming train be full?
Will the train arrive at all?

Will I last 'til evening falls
And this caravan recalls?
'Cross the car park foghorns sounding,
Eerily the conscious hounding,

Echoes of a world outside
Without angst, just time and tide,
Friendly faces, friendly places,
Where the wind but sometimes races,

Where the workload shifts with seasons,
Need, not greed, commands the reasons,
Where each creature highly ranks
And the river owns the banks…

Here I stand, in patience, waiting.
Pond'ring my importance rating.

RH

## SILENCES AND SOUND

The leaves turn: yellow and red,
gold and brown.
There is a sadness hereabouts:
the robin's autumn song is tenuous:
a vow, like gossamer, like frost.
Think of winter and you'll know
the sound I mean:
a plough through dark earth,
seagulls crying,
scintillations of ice,
freezing fog.
Where now the songs of spring?
The leaves sidle in silence: drift and fall,
fathom and float.
Not here the lofted call of larks in blue:
only the ringing strands of frosted silk;
tension, glitterings.
Mist and attendant memory, whispers, shrouds:
The snowdrops are buried deep;
not a hint of anything, only fog,
wood smoke.
Brown leaves and gold, red and yellow,
splinters of ice:
toadstools lift their tonsures, resound
In the silence, like faith.
Funereal the robin's song - its threnody.
Singing without solace, a dirge, notes that spin
their radial geometries.
What appals more than this? Snowfall?
Slants of rain? Clouds?
Diagonals of light, coruscate, shimmer:
The robin's song is thinner than it sounds
And down the air, the silences impinge.

ML

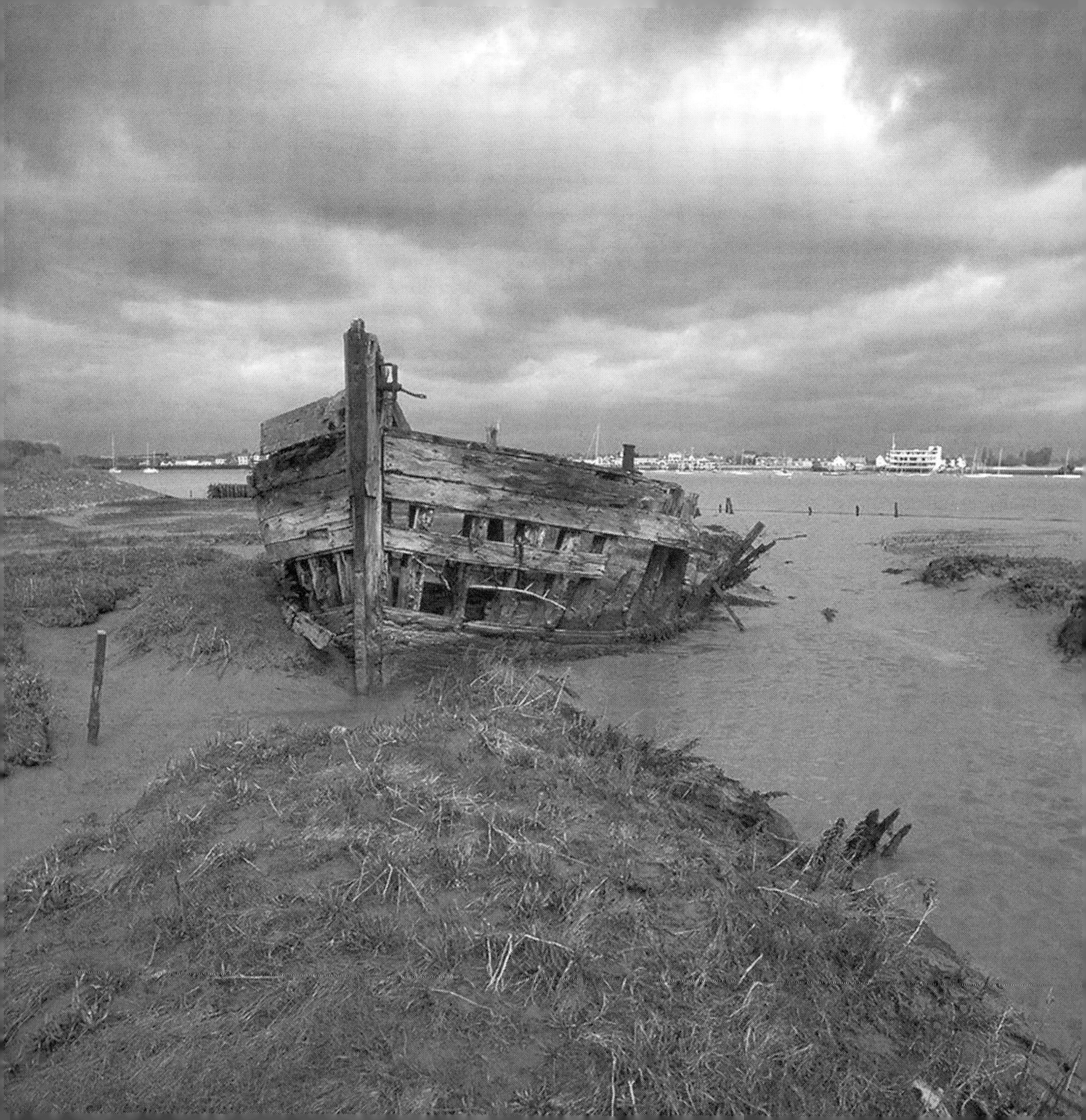

## REDSHANK AT DAWN

When dawn and I up-rise as one together:
when my early morning

sleepless

silver eyes

open to the sheen of these bright flats
and the seabirds cry their critical aubade
against the dark

- then light is possible -

When the widgeon with a whistle
that denies the blackest thoughts
hurl the fading stars into the blue

- of stellar absence -

and the vessels on their chains across the tide
slew in silent circles that describe
the square of time

then I am timeless.

When H2° of E and $MC^2$
refuse to bow their calculus to Him
who rises in sublimity and robes
of trailing gold.

ML

Where I on life's frail altar of the self
sacrifice the essence of my soul
to silts and saltings

- then what's defined? -

and if a definition could resolve
the daily rise and fall of this wide sea -
the twice absolved redemption of the moon
that nightly gleans its glory from the sun

then would the dawn's emergence
- night's demise -

be any more or less the cold concern
of these resplendent redshank in the text
of this confession?

Forgive
me Father
I have surely
sinned

and here beside the story of the Thames:
protagonist or priest without a church -

I celebrate this thoughtless ebbing tide
that preaches the duality of sight
with all the glare and glitter
- so allied -
to this denouement

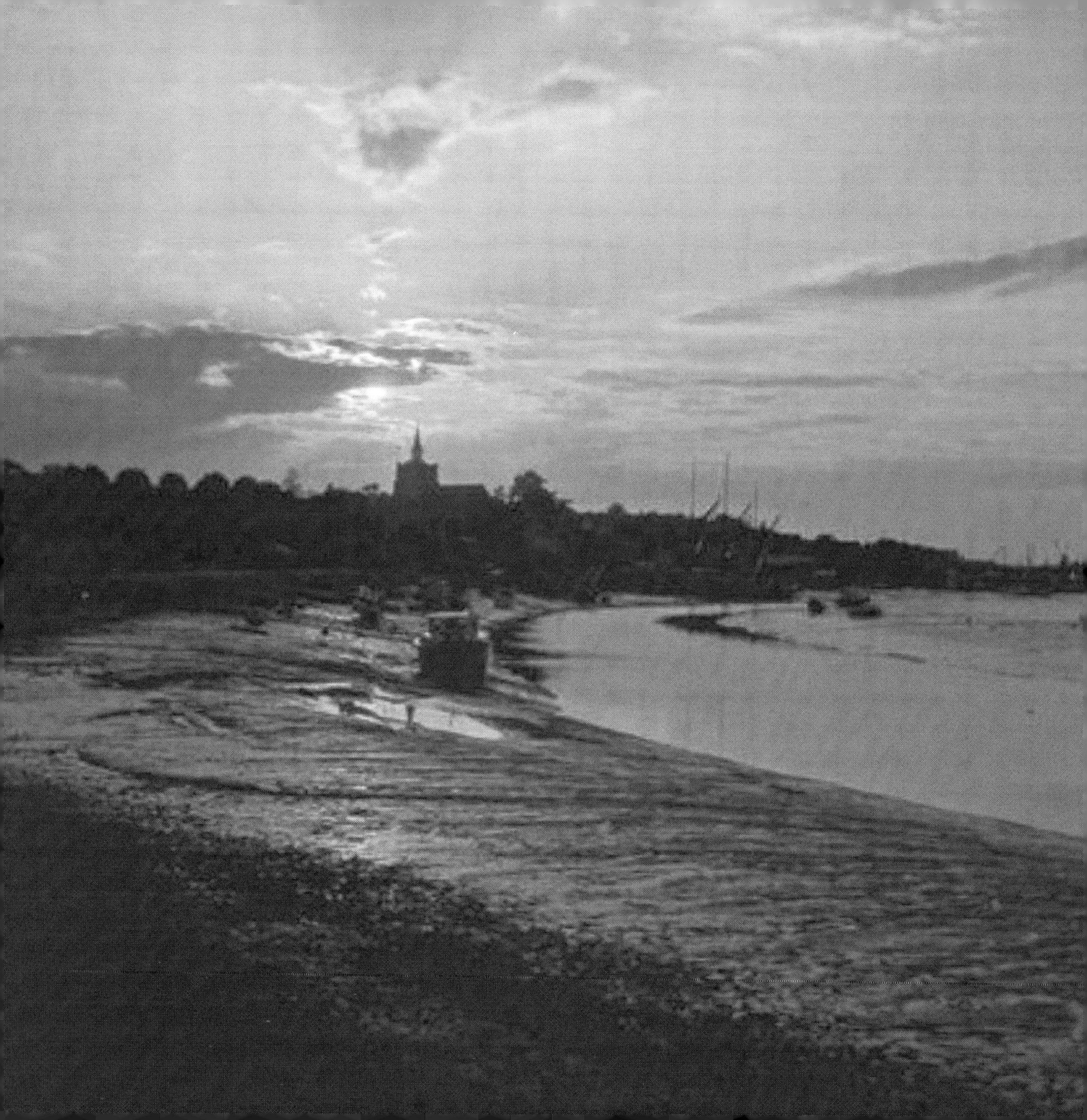

## NORTHEY LAMENT

When evening falls on Northey Isle,
Where goose and gull and snipe beguile -
You step through time and rest awhile -
Reflect on Byrhtnoth's fall.

Are mud-banks really what they seem?
You close your eyes on Panta's stream.
Is that a war cry in your dream,
Or curlews' plaintive call?

And do you see a giant stand
Erect and proud with sword in hand,
Determined to defend the land
For kith and kin and friend?

Is that the sound of spear on shield,
The taunts of men, too proud to yield
To Viking force upon that field?
Or echoes in the wind?

Is that the eagle, carrion-wise,
That soars in ghoulish enterprise
The half-dome of the Essex skies,
All memory to rescind?

The heroes of the slaughter-place
Left not a sign, nor hint, nor trace.
The bloom of Anglo-Saxon race
Here found its tragic end...

RH

## GLAUCOUS GOLD

There is a land that has a Saxon heart
Where language of the Latinate is least,
Where Nordic on a tongue of salt is cast
On level lines towards the northern seas.
And there am I, a pilgrim on the shore,
Abandoned by the stars that were my home
To form or fail, by what unwritten law
That leaves a man such solitudes to roam?
This ooze, that in the miracle of light
Can seem as though eternity in time,
Will sudden turn to dark on lowering sky
And leave the soul, so desolate, so blind.
And yet, these bleak horizons hold me still,
No risen scarp can move my leaden faith;
No undulating wealth of upland fields
Could buy the rich seclusion of this place.
This glaucous gold is all that I could wish,
The spirit's voice on skeins of endless geese;
Alluvial, the thought that through the mist
Attaches shape to solitary trees.
So here I wait the memory of tides
Where curlew call like echoes of the past
And over top the heron ghostly glides
Across the wide and moon-suffusive marsh.

ML

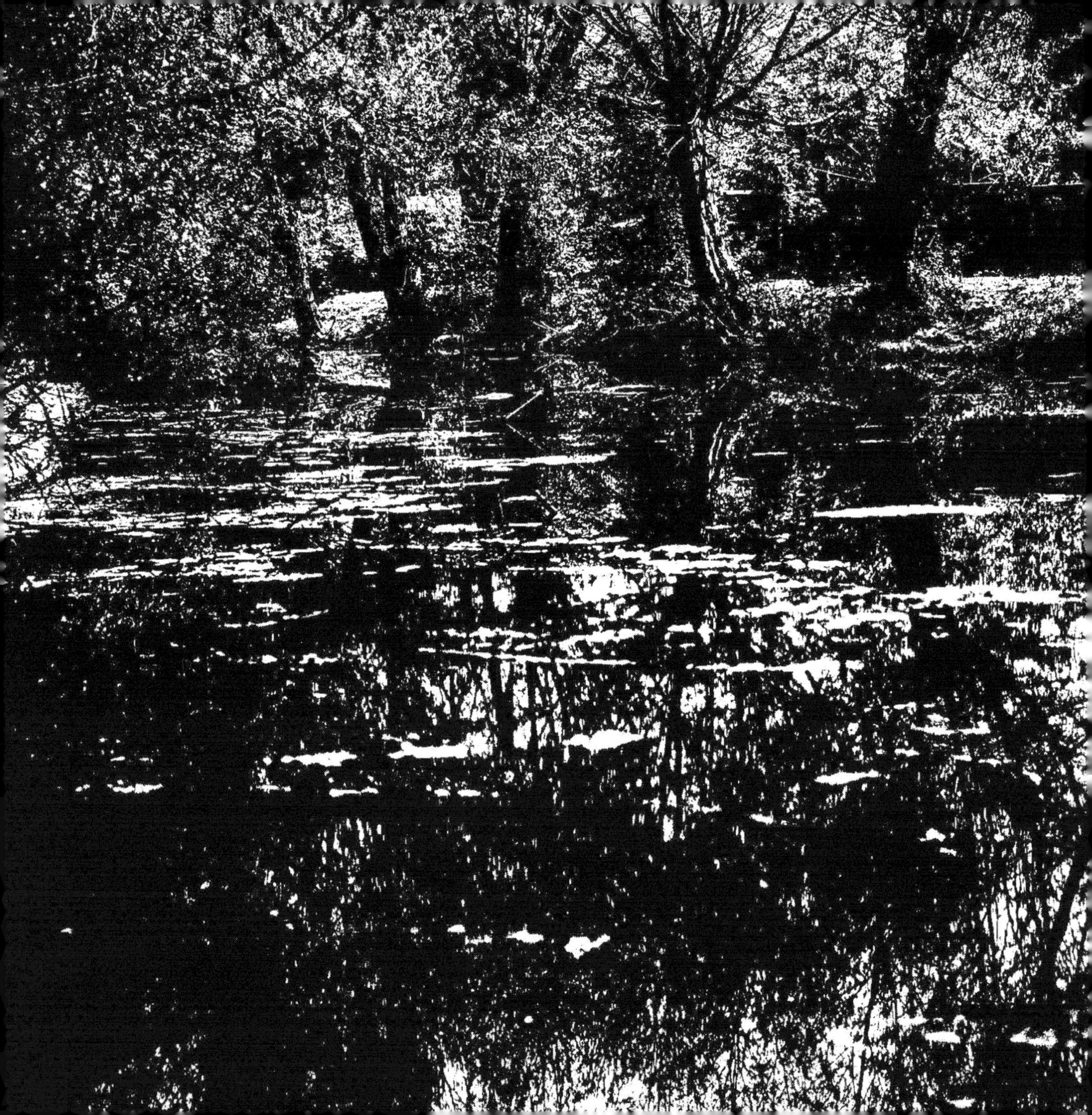

**CASTLE MOUNT**

On Rayleigh's Mount I walked that summer morning,
It's one-time moat alive with ducks and coots.
The coppiced willows, ivy-grown, adorning,
The busy vole at home among their roots.

A pigeon cooed, the magpie homed in splendour,
As birdsong all about joined in the throng
To drown the voice from car and train and vendor.
The redbreast sang. The raven croaked along.

A sound-swell rose up in my contemplation
From fosse and bailey, barbican and ditch
And I heard voices in its congregation
In Saxon tongues and some of Norman pitch.

From far in time commands and curses tumbled.
The sounds of horses, anvil, craftsmen's toil.
A blessing mixed with serfs' and yeomans' grumbles.
A minstrel's song. A sermon of the soil.

And tears and laughter mixed with lamentation.
The voice of Sweyn, the Conqueror's kin, resounds.
And England's Standard Bearers proudly take their station
And raise their banners on this humble mount.

RH

**CLODS**

Recently, I was given the name; ‘clay-kicker’,
not as an insult, you understand,
    nor taken as such.

    If as a child
you’d walked the Essex fields,
you’d know exactly, what was meant.

I can still remember the weight:
the clodded feet,
grown to enormous size -
impediment to every step.

I thought I was a giant:
fee-fo-fumming in the wind -
showered with autumn from exploding elms.

When it got too heavy
you gave a kick and away it flew,
great glutinous lumps spattering the furrows.

All in vain though, a few more steps
and you were back where you started -
    a diminutive clod-’opper,
wearing the weather, like your father’s shoes.

ML

## PARTIAL SOLAR ECLIPSE OVER ESSEX

(11 August 1999)

Through the darkened glass I watched them,
Moon-shaped sun and sun-shaped moon.
Mystic battle of the heavens in the hours towards noon.

Through the darkened glass I watched them,
Moon's incursion, blotting sun
As the battle of the heavens dimmed the light and moonlight won

Briefly, as the seer promised.
People hushed, in awe, aghast
While the moon's intrepid shadow on its progress flaunted past.

Yet the moon for all his effort
Could not match the Victor's style;
Only in the elder shadows triumphed he a little while.

Underneath those midnight berries
Shadow play, an eerie sight –
Moon-shaped sunbeams echoed crescents, mirrors of the source of light.

Through the darkened glass I watched them,
Moon-shaped sun and sun-shaped moon.
Mystic battle of the heavens in the hours towards noon.

RH

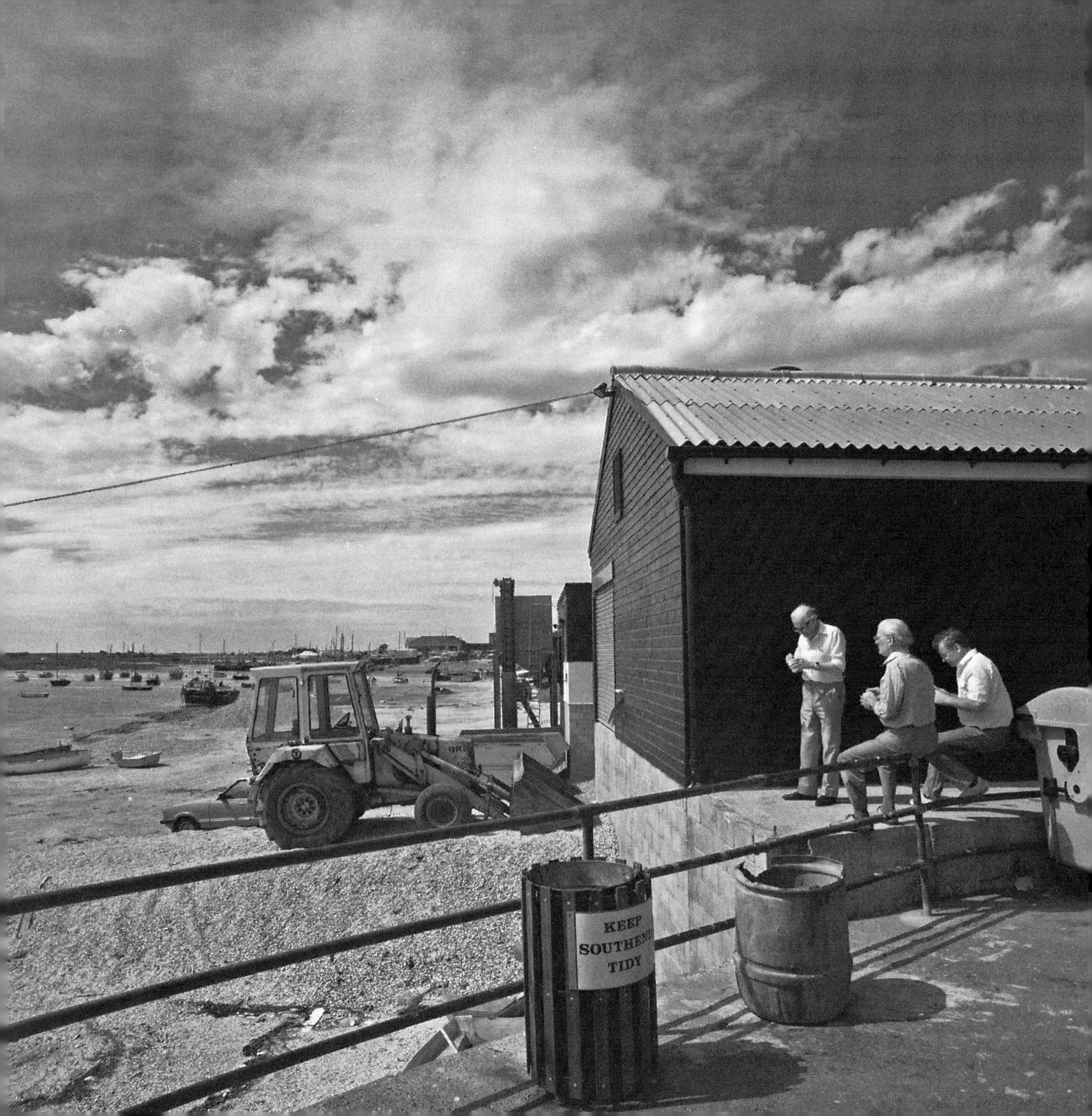
KEEP
TIDY

## COCKLE-MEN

They know the sea round here:
the creeks and gullies hidden underneath -
their tortuous meanderings.

To most, all looks the same,
  - just sea -

but to these without a chart to see them home
or gimbals and a compass to direct them -
  there is no problem.

Just like the geese that cruise that other sea
beneath the 'Plough', the 'Pleiades', 'Orion',
they set their course by instinct
  and by habit

and harbour
in their bones
the very whiteness:

  the gravity,
    the phases
      and the tides

        that moonlight
      drags around
    the cold ecliptic
and their minds.

ML

## TERPSICHORE'S JOY

She danced in the snow close to midnight –
First snow of the winter this year.
All alone in the night, with no audience there,
She ignored the wind as it tousled her hair,
With her toes cold and bare and her arms in the air,
She just danced in the snow close to midnight.

She danced in the snow close to midnight,
When like her it was fresh and new.
She ignored the hour, the squall as it blew,
All alone in the night out on tip-toe she flew –
In a ballet of grace, like a lamb in fresh dew.
She just danced in the snow close to midnight.

She danced in the snow close to midnight,
Not a care as she swerved, dipped and rose.
And with snow on her toes, in her hair, on her nose,
She was Terpsichore, gentle and glowing and bright…
And her feet barely touched the ground in her flight.
From my window I watched her abundant delight

As she danced in the snow close to midnight.

RH

## THAMES WINTER SUNSET

Just for a moment the setting sun
Set the dark dominant cloud on fire.
Solar arson. The end of mankind?
The rising of Phoenix from mist and mire?
        Should I seek sanctuary?

Though not for long. A forceful blast
Pushed close the gap and the fire burst ebbed
As soon as it spread. It couldn't last,
Leaving earth bereaved, mourning, as heaven wept.
        And I seek sanctuary.

Battle of giants! The light fights back.
Afterglow, haltingly, spreads its last chances.
Dying embers. A red glow on black.
Echoes of crimson in faltering dances.
        And I seek sanctuary.

A velvet sheen dissects the land.
Light wavers. Lingers. Mute the flaming story.
The shimmer stays upon the river's band
But fleetingly – a memory of glory.
        And I found sanctuary.

RH

## AFTER THE SUNLIGHT AND THE BLUE

when the sky is black and punctured by the stars
and the moon, like a silent scream,
rounds its up-risen lips
to a muted rictus

you will hear, if the frost allows,
the widgeons' after Christmas eerie whistle
    across the marshes

  and when the swans
as white as drifting snow
fly over silvered mudflats and the sea
with wings that also whistle and deceive
    the listening ear

you will touch the zero sentience of bone and
know the words of winter when it speaks of
ice and geese and tides as cold as stone
    or frozen mica.

ML

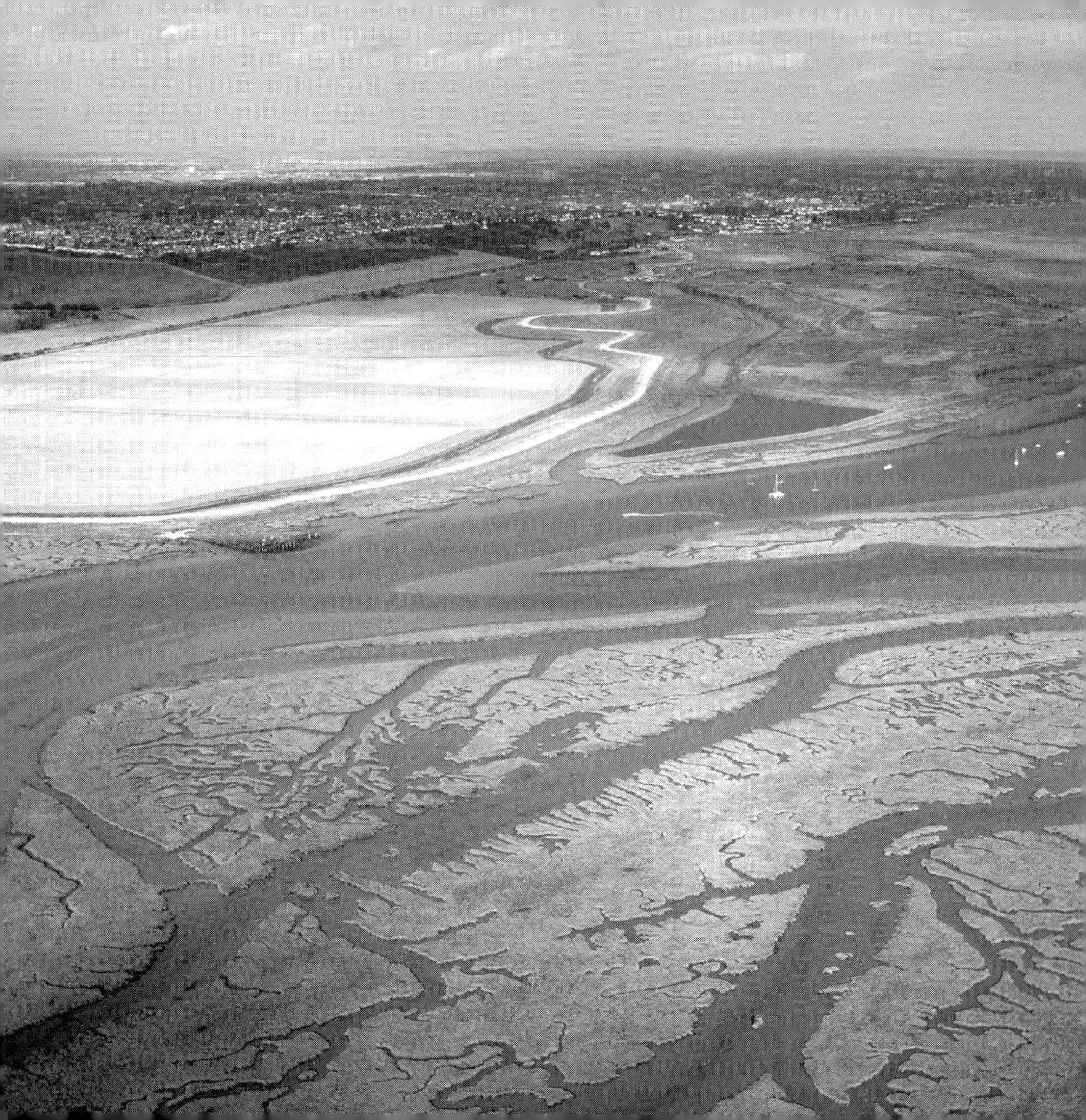

## THE RAINBOW

All the world was damp and dreadful.
Clouds were weeping sad and fretful.
Then one sunbeam, disrespectful,
Pierced the brooding sky.
And with that the mood was lifted.
Glorious arc, with colours gifted
Stood, where mists and vapour drifted,
Turning mud to gold.

And the land about recovered.
Skylark sang and kestrel hovered.
People smiled at one another,
Not afraid to cry.
Helping, not too cowed to bother,
Paused with honour in their race,
Reached and touched another's space,
Kissed the stranger's weary face –
Compassion taking hold.

RH

## A WHIMBREL IN APRIL

Is this a whimbrel, here, at Leigh on Sea
creeping amongst the saltings
and the showers?

The time of year is right for passage migrants
journeying from Africa to the Shetlands.

Like the man digging for bait along the tideline
the whimbrel is alone –

an isolate example of its species
between the oystercatchers and their bleeping
and the curlew as they bubble over gullies, sandbanks
and the Middle Grounds and ooze.

A rainbow curves and frames the spectral instant
before the wondrous prism of my eyes
and suddenly the world is just a whimbrel
and saltings and the sunlight and the mudflats
all molten like the magma
in my mind.

ML